ANCIENT JEWISH COINS

BY

A. REIFENBERG

FOURTH EDITION

RUBIN MASS / JERUSALEM / 1965

Distributed by
ARGONAUT INC., PUBLISHERS
737 North Michigan Avenue
Chicago, Illinois 60611

Printed in Israel by "Da'ath" Press, Jerusalem

PREFACE TO THE FIRST EDITION.

The last general treatise on Jewish coins in a European language was published twenty-five years ago. In the meantime not only have some important finds been made, but investigations in Palestine and elsewhere have thrown new light on the development of Jewish art. Both these facts were fully taken into account in the present monograph. A number of unknown Jewish coins are published here for the first time and some new attributions of coins are suggested. Although strictly speaking, the coins of the Herodian Dynasty of Chalcis as well as those of the procurators and the Roman coins struck in Palestine commemorating the Jewish defeat, cannot be said to belong to the Jewish series, the author thought fit to include them.

The author is indebted to his friends Prof. L. A. Mayer, Prof. M. Schwabe and Dr. H. Levy of the Hebrew University for many valuable suggestions, and desires to acknowledge his gratitude to Miss E. Levin for her correction of the translation.

Jerusalem, October 1940   A. REIFENBERG

Owing to the demise of the author, the book does not include material which has come to light subsequent to the publication of the first edition.

PREFACE TO THE SECOND EDITION.

This new edition makes it possible to have a number of coins included which have been published in the meantime; other coins are published for the first time. In order to ease reference to the first edition such coins have not been provided with new numbers, but are provided with Latin letters (A, B etc.) according to their chronological sequence.

Because of their importance for Jewish numismatics a full description of a recent find of shekels is given. This find confirms the view of G. F. Hill and others that the shekels were struck during the First Revolt.

A great number of photographs has been changed in order to provide better illustrations. The author is again indebted to the Directors of the Palestine Oriental Society for their permission to use most of the plates which had originally appeared in the Journal of this Society. A number of misprints which had crept into the first edition have been corrected. In this connection the author is grateful for the advice of his friends Dr. Stella Ben-Dor and Dr. Kirschner of Jerusalem. Reviews with valuable criticism of the monograph have, of course, been taken into account and in this connection the review of F. O. Waage in the American Journal of Archaeology may be specially mentioned. There is perhaps no need to stress the fact that most valuable guidance has been derived from the masterly description of coin-types given in the British Museum Catalogue by G. F. Hill.

The author dedicates this new edition to the memory of his friend Dr. H. Levy of the Hebrew University.

Jerusalem, January, 1947   A. R.

PERSIAN PERIOD

A coin (1A) published some years ago by the author[1] is not only the oldest Hebrew coin, but is likely, however modestly, to throw some new light on one of the least known periods of Jewish history.

The coin is of archaic character. Both corners of the eye are visible as if seen enface and both reverse and obverse show the formal smile, which is generally absent from coins later than the first half of the fifth century. Both heads show a border line of pearl dots on the upper part of the head and that of the woman has the same device at the lower neck where it might also represent a necklace. Such border lines are likewise absent on Greek coins of the fifth to fourth century.[2] The hair is tied in a knot at the back, a feature which is characteristic, for instance, of Athenian coins of the late sixth to the end of the fifth century.[3]

The obverse of the coin resembles the bearded heads of the fifth century coins of Gaza,[4] and most strikingly so one on a "Philisto-Arabian" coin found in Palestine and published by Lambert,[5] who attributes it to the fifth century. Somewhat similar bearded heads are found on the coins of Lycian dynasts of the fifth century[6] and there appears to be some stylistic relationship to heads on the Persepolis rock reliefs.[7]

The female head on the reverse has likewise much in common with the Aphrodite represented on these Lycian coins[8] and on

[1] A Reifenberg: PEF QSt. Oct. 1934, pp. 100 et seq.

[2] K. Regling: Die antike Muenze als Kunstwerk (Berlin, 1924), p. 96.

[3] K. Regling, l.c., p. 36, and Pls. IV and VII.

[4] G. F. Hill: Cat. of Greek Coins in the B.M., Vol. Palestine, Pl. XIX No. 14, etc.

[5] QDAP, II, 1932, p. 1 and sq. (No. 50).

[6] F. Imhoof-Blumer: Portraitköpfe (Leipzig, 1885), Pl. III, No. 9.

[7] A. V. Pope: A Survey of Persian Art. (1938), Vol. IV, Pl. 91-93.

[8] E. Babelon: Traité. II, 2 and Pl. XCIX.

6

early coins of Cnidos.[9] Besides these, the female head on a fifth century coin of Gaza[10] may be compared to it. Palestinian "pillar Astarte" figurines, which go down to the sixth century, also show a certain relationship, although they are, of course, of much cruder workmanship.

Whilst in the case of purely Greek coins all those afore-mentioned characteristics would point to a period not later than the early fifth century, our coin, struck in a corner remote from the centres of Greek culture, most probably dates from a somewhat later period, say about the middle of the fifth century.

The inscription reads *beqa'*, i. e. "one half" the designation of a half shekel, well known from the Bible (Gen. xxiv, 22 and Exod. xxxviii, 26) and from a number of stone weights of approximately 6.1 grm.[11] found in Judaea. The engraver of the coin did not have enough space for the last letter and has therefore placed it in the middle of the head, a procedure familiar from other coins of the Persian period.[12]

The script is clearly Hebrew; the shape of the letters, however, is slightly different from those on seals, stone weights, etc., dating from the eighth to sixth centuries. The "beth" is more rounded, a feature characteristic of Phoenician coins.[13] Although somewhat similar forms of *qoph* do occur on earlier inscriptions, the letter employed here resembles most closely the archaistic writing on the late Hebrew shekels[14] and may represent a transitional form between the old Hebrew and the shekel characters. We see therefore, that the script is well in line with the chronological classification arrived at on the basis of stylistic features.

The coin weighs 3.88 grm. and as in the case of the "Philisto-Arabian" coins (3.6-4.0 grm.) the Attic standard of a

B. V. Head: *Cat. of Greek Coins in the B.M.*, Vol. *Caria*, Pl. XIV, and Regling' *l.c.*, No. 169.

[10] G. F. Hill, *l.c.*, Pl. XIX, No. 13.

[11] D. Diringer: *Le Iscrizioni Antico-Ebraiche Palestinesi* (Firenze, 1934). pp. 277 sq.

[12] M. Narkiss: *Coins of Palestine*, II (Jerusalem, 1938), Nos. 1-11, pp. 87-88 (Hebrew).

[13] B. V. Head: *Historia Numorum* (Oxford, 1911), Table IV, 7.

[14] Hill, *l.c.* Pl. XXX, and this book Pl. X.

drachm (max. 4.36 grm.) was aimed at. This introduction of the
Attic standard into Palestine is by no means astonishing. We need
not describe here the strong cultural influences of the West on
Palestine, but as an example let us only quote the import of
Greek ceramics which started in the seventh and sixth centuries
already.[15] The Athenian silver money had become almost an
international currency in the fifth century and was accepted by
both Greeks and non-Greeks in preference to all other coins.[16]
No wonder then that it was imitated, or that other coins were
struck on the same standard in many parts of the ancient world,
the "Philisto-Arabian" coins of the fifth century being but one
of many examples. Our coin serves as additional proof. We know
that in the sphere of the Attic standard the didrachm, or stater,
was the original monetary unit.[17] After the reform of Hippias
(514-511 B.C.) this didrachm weighed 8.73 grm. (max.'. Besides
it is interesting to note that the Septuaginta always translates
"shekel" as "didrachm." We, therefore, have before us half a
didrachm (light stater) or half a shekel of Attic weight.

We have seen that the coin was struck about the middle of
the fifth century. Not only because of its provenance (Hebron),
but especially because of the Hebrew inscription, the coin was
certainly minted in Palestine. It might of course have been struck
by one of the local non-Jewish rulers, as the coins of Gaza for
instance. But this possibility seems to be rather remote because
of the typical Hebrew inscription, for the people of the Philistine
cities at all events spoke a different language (Neh. xiii, 24).
Besides beqa' seems specially to denote the sacred Jewish levy,
since in Exod. xxxviii, 26 the word is so explained. ("A beka for
every man, that is, half a shekel, after the shekel of the sanctuary.")
The view that beqa' is a specifically Jewish word is furthermore
supported by the fact that all stone-weights bearing this inscription
were found in Judaea proper.[18]

---

[15] J. H. Iliffe, QDAP, II, 1932, p. 15.

[16] B. V. Head, l.c., p. 373; besides an early fifth century coin of Aegae
was found at Atlit (Lambert, l. c. p. 2) and fourth century coins of Attic
standard in numerous other instances.

[17] Pauly-Wissowa: Realenzyklopädie. s.v. "Stater," p. 2,176.

[18] Diringer, l.c. pp. 277 sq.

The heathen character of the coin of this period in no way disproves the assumption that the coin was struck by a Jewish authority, since not only seals of the eighth to sixth centuries, but also the "Yehud" coins[19] of the fourth century (Nos. 1-3) show the same imitation of heathen representations. Even the Talmud did not take offence at this procedure when describing the "coins of Jerusalem" as having human representations on them[20] and the Midrash[21] curiously enough describes a "current coin of Mordechai", which shows Mordechai on the one side and Esther on the other.

In assuming that our coin comes from a Jewish mint, we can think of only one person who could have enjoyed the right of coinage at that time, namely Nehemiah, who was sent to Palestine in 445 as governor of Judaea. True enough, there may have been Jewish governors after Zerubbabel (Neh. v, 15), but apparently this post was abolished by the Persians in the fifth century, since there was no governor when Ezra came to Jerusalem in 458 B.C. On the other hand, Nehemiah had no immediate successor.[22] He had the full powers of a governor, best illustrated by the fact that he was even allowed to rebuild the walls of Jerusalem. Although subordinated to the satrap of Abar-Nahara (Beyond the River), it is quite plausible that Nehemiah's powers were such as to allow of the minting of coins. A parallel is found in other parts of the Persian Empire, where the internal administration was left in the hands of local dynasts under the supreme authority of the satrap, as e.g. Lycia, Cilicia, etc. In all such places[23, 24] not only the satraps, but also the local dynasts or the municipalities had the right of coinage. A further example is afforded by the aforementioned coins of Gaza.[25]

The following coins of the Persian period (1-3) were first

[19] E. L. Sukenik, *JPOS*, XIV (1934), pp. 178 et seq. and XV (1935), pp. 341 et seq.

[20] *Baba Qama* 97b.

[21] *Midrash Esther Rabba*, 129d.

[22] H. Zucker: *Studien zur Jüd. Selbstverwaltung im Altertum* (Berlin, 1936), pp. 19 et seq.

[23] Head, *l.c.* p. 688.

[24] Head, *l.c.* p. 715.

[25] Hill, *l.c.* pp. lxxxiii et seq.

correctly read by E. L. Sukenik.[26] They bear the inscription Jehud, the official Aramaic name of the province Judaea in Persian time, a designation known from the books of Daniel and Ezra[27] and from the Elephantine papyri.[28] According to Sukenik, these coins prove that Judaea enjoyed the priviliges of an autonomous province, a fact which is further substantiated by one of the coins (No. 2) seemingly bearing the name of a Jewish High-priest. On the other hand, these coins may have been issued under the authority of one of the Persian satraps.

These coins are likewise related in style to the so-called "Philisto-Arabian" coins[29] and not only the owl on Nos. 1 and 2, but also the Corinthian helmet and the mask on No. 3 show the Greek influence. The coins were struck in the 4th century some time before the victory of Alexander the Great.

Coin No. 2 was found at the excavation of Beth Zur in Southern Palestine and Sellers and Albright[30] read the name of Hezekiah on it. This Hezekiah may have been the High-priest and friend of Ptolemy I, whom we know from Josephus.[31] The inscription to the left was read in different ways, but we agree with Sukenik, that it contains most likely the elements of the name Jehud.

No. 3 is said to have been found at Gaza and forms part of the collection of the British Museum. Owing to an earlier theory held by various authors that the inscription is to be read Yahu the latter has given rise to many speculations.[32] The figure on the reverse, described here according to Hill,[33] should be compared with coins of Persian satraps, which show the Baal of Tarsus. Even on coins of Alexander the Great, and his successors Zeus is shown similarly holding an eagle in his hand.

---

[26] E. L. Sukenik, l. c. (19).

[27] Dan. 2^{25}; 5^{18}; 6^{14}; Ezra 5^1 and ^{8}; 7^{14}.

[28] A. Cowley, Aramaic Papyri of the 5th Century, Oxford 1923.

[29] G. F. Hill, l. c. (4), pp. 176 et seq.

[30] O. R. Sellers and W. F. Albright, BASOR, No. 43, 1931.

[30] O. R. Sellers: The Citadel of Beth-Zur, Philadelphia 1933, (p. 73).

[31] Contra Apionem I, 187-189.

[32] The literature is conveniently given by Sukenik, l.c., 1934.

[33] Hill, l.c., p. 181, No. 29.

THE MACCABEAN DYNASTY

In 138 B.C. a decree was issued by Antiochos VII,[1] which is of the greatest importance for Jewish numismatics, since it accorded to the Jews the right to strike coins of their own. The decree reads: "King Antiochus to Simon the High-priest and prince of his nation, and to the people of the Jews, greeting: Forasmuch as certain pestilent men have usurped the kingdom of our fathers, and my purpose is to challenge it again, that I may restore it to the old estate, and to that end have gathered a multitude of foreign soldiers together, and prepared ships of war, my meaning also being to go through the country that I may be avenged of them that have destroyed it, and made many cities in the kingdom desolate; now therefore I confirm unto thee all the oblations which the kings before me granted thee, and whatsoever gift besides they granted. *I give thee leave also to coin money for thy country with thine own stamp and as concerning Jerusalem and the sanctuary, let them be free;* and all the armour that thou hast made, and fortresses, that thou has built, and keepest in thine hands, let them remain unto thee. And if anything be, or shall be, owing to the king, let it be forgiven thee from this time forth for evermore. Furthermore, when we have obtained our kingdom, we will honour thee, and thy nation and thy temple, with great honour, so that your honour shall be known throughout the world."

As against W i l l r i c h,[2,3] there is no reason to doubt the authenticity of this decree. B i c k e r m a n n[4] points out that the absence of coins generally attributed to Simon during excavations at Beth Zur[5] and Bethel[6] is no proof to the contrary.

With the exception of No. 6 all the coins generally attributed to Simon are of the utmost rarity and at Beth-Zur e.g. only three

[1] I Macc. 15: 2-9.

[2] H. Willrich: *Urkundenfälschungen in der hellenistisch-jüdischen Literatur,* 1924.

[3] H. Willrich, *Ztsch. f. alttestamentliche Wissenschaft,* 1933, p. 79.

[4] E. Bickermann: *Der Gott der Makkabäer,* 1937.

[5] O. R. Sellers: *The Citadel of Beth Zur,* 1933. (cf. also O. R. Sellers and W. F. Albright, *BASOR,* 1931, No. 43, p. 13).

[6] W. F. Albright: *BASOR,* 1934, No. 56, p. 14.

coins of the later Maccabean period were found although such coins are most common. The rarity of the bronze coins usually attributed to Simon is easily explained by the short lapse of time between the grant of Antiochus and the death of Simon.

On the other hand there are various other reasons which point to an attribution of these coins to the period of the first revolt. It is e.g. strange to think that the coinage of Simon's successors should be much poorer than his own. Besides, the cup on No. 3 is not only identical with the cup represented on the shekels of the first revolt (Nos. 137 etc.) but Pick[7] points out that their fabric, the planchets being flat, is also similar. Notwithstanding these facts we, nevertheless, prefer to attribute these coins to Simon until new numismatic evidence is forthcoming.

1. SIMON MACCABAEUS (143/2—136/5 B.C.).

There was no understanding between Judaism and the ideas of Hellenism which penetrated the Orient after the victory of Alexander the Great. Both in exile and under the rule of its priests the Jewish people had become conscious of its historic mission. The national God had become the one and only God of the Universe and the Jews regarded themselves as His chosen interpreters. Nowhere in the ancient world was there any resistance against Hellenism but in Judaea. The revolt started primarily because of the existence of a Jewish party which tried to reconcile the conflicting ideas, and Bickermann[8] has shown that the persecution under Antioches Epiphanes is to be explained by the assimilatory tendencies of the ruling class in Jerusalem. The coins struck by Antiochos IV in the different cities of his Empire at the outbreak of the revolt (168/169 B.C.) clearly show that there was nowhere a tendency to replace the native gods by the cult of Zeus. The Maccabees, however, felt that no reconciliation whatsoever between Greek polytheism and Jewish monotheism was possible; they succeeded in their revolt against the spread of Hellenism in Judaea and in this way they preserved monotheism for Judaism and the world.

The rule of the Maccabees opens a new chapter in the history

[7] B. Pick, *Numismatic Review*, Vol II. No. 4, pp. 5 et seq. 1945.
[8] E. Bickermann: *Der Gott der Makkabäer*, 1937.

of the Jewish people. The safeguarding of their political independence provided for an undisturbed inner development which found its outward expression also in art. For the first time in Jewish history no foreign artistic models are adopted, but specific Jewish objects are represented. In 142 B.C. the "yoke of the heathens was thrown off" and the people started to date its documents in "the first year of Simon, the high-priest, commander and leader of the Jews." As pointed out above, Simon was granted the right to strike coins in 139 B.C. although apparently he only made use of this privilege in the fourth year of his reign, a not uncommon procedure as shown by Hill.[9]

The coins show the national feeling of the time.[10, 11] Although the early Hebrew writing had dropped out of use long ago, the coins were nevertheless stamped in the ancient script, a procedure followed in all the issues of the later rulers apart from the Herodians, who used Greek writing, as will be shown later. The same Simon, of whom it is said that "he augmented the sacred vessels of the temple" proceeded also to their representation on the coins. Not only do we find on his coins the chalice used for wine-offering (No. 6), but also the *lulab* (bundle of twigs) and *ethrog* (citrus fruit), the symbols of the feast of Tabernacles. Besides, a basket full of fruits is depicted (No. 4), in all probability an allusion to the offerings of the first-fruits. The palm-tree on the reverse of this coin became in later times a symbol of the country, of which Plinius says: "Judaea vero incluta est vel magis palmis". With all these symbols we meet again at later periods, when synagogal art was at its highest level.[12] It may be mentioned that analysis shows these coins to be of excellent quality, containing over 80% of copper.[13]

[9] G. F. Hill: *Cat. of Greek Coins in the British Museum: Palestine*, p. xciv.

[10] It should nevertheless again be pointed out that the attribution of these coins to Simon is questionable.

[11] For a detailed study of Jewish symbols on coins see: P. Romanoff: *Jewish Symbols on Ancient Jewish coins* (Philadelphia, 1944).

[12] A. Reifenberg: *Denkmäler der jüdischen Antike*, 1937, p. 41-42.

[13] A. Reifenberg: *Ztsch. d. deutschen Palästina-Vereins*, 1927, pp. 175 et seq.

2. JOHN HYRCANUS (135-104 B.C.).

In pre-Maccabean times the government of the Jews was a hierocracy, and a high-priest acted as leader at the head of it. Whereas in earlier times the high-priest was but a commissioner of the king, he succeeded in the third century to achieve a princely position. In the course of time the high-priest dissociated himself from the Jewish clergy and in the second century he is called by Jesus Sirach[14] a prince, "who looks after his people against robbery and fortifies his city against a siege".[15]

John Hyrcanus not only knew how to obtain extraordinary success against the declining Seleucid rulers, but also succeeded in strengthening the princely might of the high priest over the pharisaic gerousia. It is a proof of the growing princely consciousness that he was the first Jewish ruler to have his name stamped on coins. The gerousia of the scribes sinks into insignificance[16]; it is not mentioned on the coins, on which appears solely the name of the community of the Jews as a whole, since we know this to be the correct meaning of the word חבר.[17] On some coins John seems to designate himself as the leader of this community. (Nos. 7 and 11).

We have to thank Harry J. Stein[18] for the observation, that on some of the coins Greek letters appear in the lower left field below the cornucopiae. The letters discovered up to now are "A" (No. 9b), "M" and "Pi" Stein proposes these letters to be the initials of magistrates charged with the striking of coins, the letter "A" to stand for "Aristobulus", the son and successor of John Hyrcanus.

The Greek letter "A" on the obverse of No. 8 has not yet been satisfactorily explained. Madden[19] thought the letter to refer to the king's alliance with Alexander Zabinas in 128 B.C. Stein now makes the suggestion that the coins were minted

[14] Jesus Sirach, 50⁴.

[15] E. Bickermann, l.c., p. 57-58.

[16] H. Zucker: Studien zur jüdischen Selbstverwaltung im Altertum, 1936, p. 47-48.

[17] Schürer: Gesch. des Jüdischen Volkes, I, p. 269.

[18] H. J. Stein, Num. Review, I, No. 2. pp. 19 et seq. 1943.

[19] F. W. Madden: Coins of the Jews, 1881, p. 81.

after the death of John Hyrcanus and that the "A" stands for Aristobulus, who, when only a magistrate, had the same letter minted on the reverse as described above.

The symbol of cornucopiae was most common on coins of Seleucid kings and it was probably from this coinage that John Hyrcanus adopted it. It may be mentioned that as the coins of Simon so the coins of John are minted from good bronze, showing a copper content of about 83%. On many of them the inscription is incomplete, only the beginning of the legend being given correctly.

3. JUDAS ARISTOBULUS (104-103 B.C.)

According to Josephus,[20] Aristobul was the first Maccabean ruler to adopt the title of king, but this statement is not corroborated by his coins. On the coins (Nos. 13 and 13a) he is only styled "high-priest", and Strabo[21] may be right in stating that only the successors of Aristobul assumed the royal title. On the other hand, it is quite possible that the coins were struck in the beginning of his reign, when he had not yet assumed the title of king. The scarcity of his coins is easily explained by the fact, that his reign lasted one year only.

4. ALEXANDER JANNAEUS (103-76 B.C.).

Alexander Jannaeus was the first Maccabean ruler to style himself King on his coins and he was the first to stamp his name and title also in Greek.

The classification of his coins which we give here is mainly based on a hoard discovered during excavations on Mt. Ophel near Jerusalem which was published by Lambert.[22] There were over 300 coins of the anchor wheel type (No. 14) in this hoard, and apart from some coins of the same type, but of smaller denomination (No. 15), eight coins struck by John Hyrcanus were found. From this find the conclusion may be drawn that the smaller denomination was actually struck by Alexander, and not by his successors as was previously assumed. Further, the pre-

[20] *Ant.* XIII, 11, 1; *BJ.* I, 3, 1.
[21] Strabo, XVI, 2,40.
[22] C. Lambert, *PEF. QSt.* 1927. p. 184 *et seq.*

sence of some coins struck by John Hyrcan seems to prove that the anchor-wheel types were the first to be struck by Alexander. None of the anchor-flower types (No. 16) were found, but since these coins show the same inscription as those mentioned above, it is to be assumed that these coins are a later issue of Alexander Jannaeus. The small denomination belonging to this type is probably represented by No. 17. The comparative rarity of the anchor-flower type is probably to be explained by the fact that all available coins of this type were overstruck by his successor, as will be shown later. The representation of an anchor on his coins, if not simply borrowed from Seleucid coins, may perhaps be an allusion to his conquest of Jaffa and other ports of the Mediterranean. The wheel may be connected with solar ideas; in later times it is often found in the decoration of the synagogues.[23] There is no doubt, according to M a d d e n,[24] that two coins of the anchor-wheel type bear the inscription ΒΑΣΙΛΙΣ ΑΛΕΞΑΝΔ, which means that they were struck by Queen Alexandra, the wife of Alexander Jannaeus. But because Hill[25] expresses grave doubts as to the accuracy of this reading and because the Hebrew inscription is illegible on both coins, we decided not to include them in this monograph.

5. JONATHAN HYRCANUS II (67 AND 63-40 B.C.).

As early as 1867 M e r z b a c h e r[26] attributed the coins with cornucopiae and the title "Jonathan the High-Priest" to Jonathan Hyrcanus II, an attribution discarded by all later authors. S c h ü r e r[27] considers this hypothesis quite possible, but absolutely uncertain, since nothing is known about the Hebrew name of Hyrcanus. On numismatic grounds, however, we hold that not only these coins, büt also the anchor-flower coins of Alexander restruck with the title "Jonathan the High-Priest" (No. 18) actually belong to Hyrcanus II and not to Alexander.

Notwithstanding all the difficulties which Alexander had in

---

[23] A. Reifenberg, *l. c.* (12), p. 20-21.
[24] F. W. Madden, *l.c.*, pp. 91-92.
[25] G. F. Hill, *l.c.*, p. xcv; cf. also Kahrstedt, *Klio,* 1910, pp. 284 *et seq.*
[26] E. Merzbacher, *Ztsch. f. Numismatik,* Vol. III, 1876, pp. 201 *et seq.*
[27] E. Schürer, *l.c.*, I, p. 285.

dealing with the Pharisees the general assumption that he himself ordered his coins to be restruck seems to be most improbable. Alexander had never denounced his royal dignity and there is no precedent for a ruler crossing out his royal title for political reasons. Besides, the presence of a number of coins not restruck, however small, tells against such a hypothesis. On the other hand it is very likely that the royal title was overstruck by his successor, Hyrcanus II, who already held the pontificial office in the lifetime of his mother. This was probably not done during the first part of his reign, which only lasted four months, and after wich he renounced royal and pontifical dignity in favour of his brother Aristobulus II (67 B.C.). But in 63, not only Aristobulus and Hyrcanus II appeared before Pompeius but also delegates of the people, and the latter asked Pompeius for the restitution of the priestly rule of former days. The final decision was given in the same year. The autonomous Jewish district being considerabely reduced, its rule was conferred upon Hyrcanus II, but only with the title of High-Priest and without the title of King.[28] During his rule (63-40 B.C.), the coins of Alexander were probably restruck with the pontificial title and corresponding coins freshly issued. There seem to exist no coins issued by Aritobulus II, the pontificial title making the attribution of No. 13 to Aristobulus I fairly certain.

We hold that not only the coins bearing the inscription Jonathan (Nos. 18, 19), but also the coins bearing the name in the form of Jehonathan (No. 20) were struck by Jonathan Hyrcanus II. It is most risky to jump to far reaching conclusions on the strength of the different ways of spelling the theophoric name, as did Lambert,[29] Marmorstein[30] and Narkiss,[31] who, attributing these coins to Alexander Jannaeus, thought the difference due to party-strife with the Pharisees. Both ways of spelling occur not only on these coins, but also on the coins previously issued by Alexander.[31] Besides, both ways of writing

[28] Josephus, *Ant.* XIV, 4,4; *BJ.* I, 7,6-7 and especially *Ant.* XX, 10.
[29] C. Lambert, *l. c.* (22).
[30] A. Marmorstein, *PEF QSt.* 1928, pp. 48 *et seq.*
[31] M. Narkiss, *Bulletin of the Jewish Palestine Exploration Society* I, 1934, pp. 10 *et seq.*

ₛuch theophoric names occur side by side on a sepulchral inscription of the first century B.C. and on many other inscriptions.[32]

In case D e r e n b o u r g is right in his identification, a cor-
roboration of Hyrcan's Hebrew name being Jannai, the equival-
ent of Jonathan, is given in Talmudic sources.[33]

6. ANTIGONUS MATTATHIAS (40-37 B.C.).

Antigonus, whose Hebrew name we only know from his
coins, came to the throne in 40 B.C. The coins are struck from
bad metal, the copper content being less that 70% and the lead-
content exceeding 27%. This deterioration of the metal as against
the coins of his predecessors[4] has surely to be attributed to
the frequent extortions made by the Romans[35] and to the con-
tinual warfare raging at the time.

The Greek inscription on the reverse gives his royal title,
whereas on the Hebrew obverse only the pontifical title is mentioned. The Hebrew inscription is mostly incomplete and the
coins are generally very badly preserved owing to the high content of lead. On some coins the letters "אנ" seem to appear between the horns, a fact not yet satisfactorily explained.[36] N a r k i s s[37]
who reads them otherwise, considers the letters to represent
simply the abbreviation of Antigonus' title.

The emblems represented on the coins of Antigonus do
not differ generally from those on the coins of his predecessors,
meeting as we do with cornucopiae, wreath etc. But on some
of his coins, apart from a design not fully explained as yet (No.
24), we meet for the first time with the representation of the
seven-branched candlestick, wich later became the most characteristic symbol of Judaism. The form of the candlestick corresponds essentially to that represented on the arch of Titus

---

[32] S. Klein. Jüd. palästinensisches Corpus Inscriptionum, 1920, p. 14 et seq.

[33] J. Derenbourg: Essai sur l'histoire et la géographie de la Palestine, 1867,
pp. 146-148.

[34] A. Reifenberg, Z. D. P V. 1927, pp. 175 et seq.

[35] Josephus, Ant. XIV, 14,16, BJ. 1, 15,2; Dio Cassius, XLVIII, 41.

[36] Hill, l.c., p. xcv.

[37] M. Narkiss: Coins of Palestine, Part One: Jewish Coins, 1936, p. 33.

and to the many representations of this symbol in later synagogal art.[38]

The vessel represented on the obverse of No. 24 is explained by de Saulcy as the table of shew-bread, a description which can only be accepted with reserve.[39]

THE HERODIAN DYNASTY

I. HEROD I (37-4 B.C.)

Herod, the "Idumean", was the first Jewish ruler to use only Greek writing on his coins. Although inclined towards Hellenistic ideas — incidentally he was one of the greatest city-builders of his time — he nevertheless took care to avoid hurting his subjects' feelings by the representation of human figures on his coins. We find helmets, shields, fruits etc. on his coins, some of which still show a close relationship to the coinage of his predecessors. The vessel on No. 26 is not a ceremonial head-dress,[1] but a thymiaterion[2] which, like the tripod on Nos. 26 and 30-32, is most probably meant to represent vessels used in the temple cult. The eagle on No. 44 may refer to the golden eagle affixed by him to the temple and afterwards pulled down and destroyed by the people. On some of his coins of the third year (Nos. 26-29) appears the monogram ₽ which Narkiss[3] with much probability explains as short for "Trachonitis". We know that Herod received this district from Augustus in 28 B.C., three years after his having been crowned for the second time.[4] It may be, as pointed out by Narkiss, that these coins are of a later date than the small coins resembling the Maccabean coinage.

The coins of Herod show an unusually high content of tin (over 10%). Since bronzes with so high a content of tin were

---

[38] A. Reifenberg, l. c. (12), 1937.

[39] Madden, l.c., p. 102.

[1] Hill, l.c., p. xcvii.

[2] C. Watzinger: Denkmäler Palästinas II, 1935, p. 24.

[3] M. Narkiss, Bull. of the Jewish Palestine Exploration Soc. I., 1934, pp. 8 et seq

[4] BJ. I, 20,3-4.

mainly used in implements etc.[5] this lends colour to the statement of Josephus[6] that Herod had coins struck from all his treasures because of the scarcity of ready money.[7]

2. HEROD PHILIP II (4 B.C. — 34 A.D.)

Herod Philip II was the first Jewish ruler to use the effigy of the Roman Emperor on his coins, thereby gravely infringing the Jewish Law. It should, however, be borne in mind that his rule extended over districts mainly inhabited by non-Jews (Batanaea, Trachonitis, Auranitis, Gaulanitis and Paneas).

According to Hill[8] some light is thrown by coin No. 43 on the mint from which his coins were issued. This coin gives him the title of κτίστης and since Herod Philip built the city of Caesarea Philippi (Paneas), it is most probable that the coin was struck there. The building represented on the coins may possibly be the temple of Augustus founded by Herod I. From a hitherto unpublished coin (No. 37) we learn that he first struck coins in the ninth year of his reign.

3. HEROD ANTIPAS (4 B.C. — 39 A.D.).

Herod Antipas, who inherited the tetrarchy of Galilaea and Peraea from his father, avoided hurting Jewish feelings by the representation of human effigies on his coins, though on some the name of the ruling Emperor is given. However, most of the coins bear the inscription "Tiberias", which obviously points to the fact that these coins were struck at this city, built by Antipas in honour of the Emperor Tiberius.

Some coins are said to have been struck with the dates of the year 44 and 45; the correctness of the reading having been questioned, however,[9] we decided not to include them in this monograph.

---

[5] A. Neuburger: *Technik des Altertums* 1920, p. 17.

[6] *BJ.* I, 18,4.

[7] A. Reifenberg, *ZDPV*, 1927, pp. 175 *et seq.*

[8] Hill, *l.c.* p. xcvii.

[9] Schürer, *l.c.*, pp. 416 *et seq.*, where the relevant literature is full quoted; Narkiss, *l.c.*

4 HEROD ARCHELAUS (4 B.C. — 6 A.D.).

Archelaus being the only Herodian ruler with the title of "Ethnarch", the coins bearing this inscription may with certainty be attributed to him. Archelaus, reigning over distinctly Jewish districts (Judaea and Samaria), used only such emblems as would not offend religious feeling. We again meet with cornucopiae and anchor and besides, bunches of grapes, a helmet and a galley appear on his coins.

5. AGRIPPA I (A.D. 37-44).

The last Maccabees had already introduced two languages on their coins. The Herodians had used purely Greek legends, but applied different methods in different districts, that is to say they differentiated between wholly Jewish and foreign districts. Philip proved an exception since he ruled over pagan districts, but Herod took the ban on imagery into consideration and struck coins with absolutely neutral symbols. Agrippa I did exactly the same as far as Judaea proper was concerned. There he would not have dreamed of striking coins with the Imperial portrait,[10] whilst a coin struck in Caesarea even bears his own likeness (Nos. 60A and 62).

The coins No. 58 and 62 show a very plump face, though at the same time energetic, intelligent and good-natured. The big nose — as will be seen later — is a family trait. The king is wearing the diadem. Even the heir-apparent is honoured by being depicted on horse-back (No. 38). Agrippa seems to be proud of his kingly estate; on the coins he calls himself: BACIΛEYC MEΓAC, "The Great King" The expression on his face bears out the characterisation found in literary sources. In his youth he had been extravagant and lavish to a fault.[11] He seems to have been partial to drinking, for Josephus relates[12] that he picked a quarrel with Herod Antipas in Tyre over a glass of wine. In his old age he was certainly fond of dispensing charity,

---

[10] A. Reifenberg, *Portrait Coins of the Herodian Kings*, London 1935, (reprinted from the *Numismatic Circular*, 1935).

[11] Josephus, *Ant.* 18, 6, 1; 18, 8, 8.

[12] *l.c.*, 18, 6, 2

but at the same time very prodigal,[13] inasmuch as he put up sumptuous buildings for which there was no need.

The importance Agrippa attached to his kingly estate is not merely illustrated by the painful incident in Alexandria,[14] but also by the silver robe he wore at the contests in Caesarea.[15] He would not tolerate disrespect towards his person[16] (unless the story in question is but a legend). His energy and good-nature were strongly manifested towards Silas.[17] And to the scribe who reproached him for allowing the contests, he showed himself wise and conciliatory.[18] He seems to have been a keen promoter of such contests.

The coins No. 60 A[19] and No. 62 were struck in Caesarea. On these coins we find not merely an indication of the place where they were struck. but also the date, the 7th and 8th (last) year of his reign. It will be recalled that the King died in the course of the contests at Caesarea.[15] The figure on the reverse holds a rudder and palm-branch, the latter probably being a symbol of the contests. The date is legible only on these specimens and so far as the London specimen is concerned, there seems to be the question of a different coin altogether.[20, 21, 22] The date "8" corresponding to 44/45 A.D., also found on another hitherto unpublished coin (No. 61), does not contradict Josephus, according to whom Agrippa ruled 7 years, since the first year of his reign need not necessarily have been a full year.

Despite his Hellenistic leanings Agrippa took a keen interest in everything concerning the Jewish people, who held the King in grateful memory. Not only does Josephus repeatedly re-

---

[13] l.c., 19, 7. 3.

[14] Philo, In Flaccum.

[15] Josephus, Ant. 19, 8, 2; Acts of the Apostles, 12[21].

[16] Mishnah Pessachim, 57, 2.

[17] Josephus, l.c., 19. 7, 1.

[18] l.c. 19, 7, 4.

[19] E. L. Sukenik, Kedem II, p. 21, 1945.

[20] Hill, l.c.. p. 237, No. 20.

[21] A. Reifenberg, P.E.F. QSt., 1935. p. 80. and Sukenik, Kedem II, No 21, 1945.

[22] A. Reifenberg, Portrait Coins of the Herodian Kings, London 1935 [reprinted from the Num. Circ. 1935].

fer to his loyalty towards the Jewish religion, the Mishnah also relates that, in common with every pious Jew, the King brought his offering of firstlings to the Temple. When Agrippa burst into tears at the reading of the Bible words: "Thou mayest not set a stranger over thee which is not thy brother", the Jews assembled in the Temple called out: "Do not be sad Agrippa, our brother art thou, our brother art thou". To brand Agrippa as a hypocrite pure and simple seems wholly unjustified, as will also be seen by Nos. 60, 61 which have formerly not been adequately described[24, 25, 26]. Here an event in Agrippa's life is commemorated, as again on coin No. 63, on which the King is seen crowned by two females[27, 28]. The legend on this latter coin bears allusion "to some connexion between Agrippa I, the Roman people and the Senate".[28] It is therefore to be expected that on Nos. 60 and 61 too some such event of Agrippa's life is depicted. We now find the following story in J o s e p h u s:[29]

"And for the golden chain, which had been given him by Caius of equal weight with the iron chain wherewith his royal hands had been bound, he hung it up within the limits of the Temple, over the treasury, that it might be a memorial of the severe fate he had lain under, and a testimony of his change for the better; that it might be a demonstration how the greatest prosperity may have a fall, and that God sometimes raises up what is fallen down; for this chain, thus dedicated, offered a document to all men, that king Agrippa had been once bound in chains for a small cause, but recovered his former dignity again, and a little while afterwards got out of his bounds, and was advanced to be a more illustrious king than he was before". Coins Nos. 60 and 61 commemorate this event and give support to the view,[30] that J o s e p h u s' version of King Agrippa's life

[24] Madden, l.c. p. 137, No. 2.
[25] Hill, l.c. p. xcviii.
[26] A. Reifenberg, Num. Circ., Vol. XLVI, 1938, pp. 173/174.
[27] Madden, l.c., p. 136, No. 11.
[28] Hill, l.c. p. xcvii, et seq, and Pl. XLII, 10.
[29] Ant. XXIX, 6, 1. (from the translation of William Winston, London 1825).
[30] Hölscher in Pauly-Wissowa, Realenzyklopädie, col. 1987 Vol. XVIII.

was the "officially" approved one.[31] King Agrippa, naked, as prisoners are usually represented, is crowned in the presence of the Emperor. The representation of the cowering naked king shows how "God sometimes raises up what is fallen down", from which in the words of J o s e p h u s [32], "men may understand, that all that partake of human nature, how great however they are, may fall; and that those that fall may gain their former illustrious dignity again".[33]

Some coins attributted to Agrippa by M a d d e n,[34] H i l l,[35] and N a r k i s s,[36] are not included in this monograph since there is no proof whatsoever that they were issued by Agrippa. The inscription on the reverse of No. 63 was read in six different ways.[37] We give the reading of M o m m s e n [38], which according to H i l l[39], is the best.

6. HEROD OF CHALCIS (A.D. 41—48).

A traditional friendship linked the Herodians with the Imperial Roman family, a friendship which found expression on their coins by the legend "Friend of Caesar" and "Friend of the Romans". The friendship between the two dynasties went so far as to lead to Herod's descendants not merely being entrusted with the administration of purely Jewish districts but likewise with that of large pagan zones in the Near East. Tigranes, for example, a son of Herod, was made King of Armenia,

[31] I owe this suggestion to my late friend Dr. H. Levy of the Hebrew University.

[32] *Ant.* xxix, 6, 1.

[33] E. L. Sukenik (*Kedem* II, pp. 19/20, 1945) describing the scene on Nos. 60 and 61 wants to see in it a sacrifice commemorating the victory of Claudius in Britain in A.D. 43. The crouched captive below is described as the British chieftain Caratacus. Apart from everything else (cf. A. Reifenberg, *BJPES*, XI, p. 56, 1944/5) this contention is impossible, since Caratacus was only taken prisoner in A.D. 51 whereas our coin was struck in A.D. 43 44. Sukenik was, however, the first to discover the third person in the background.

[34] Madden, *l.c.*, p. 136, Nos. 3 and 4.

[35] Hill, *l.c.*, p. 238, Nos. 21 and 22.

[36] Narkiss, *l.c.*, p. 107, Nos. 43 and 44.

[37] Madden, *l.c.*, p. 137.

[38] Th. Mommsen, *Num. Ztsch.*, Vol. III, 1872, p. 449.

[39] Hill, *l.c.*, p. xcviii.

and at a later period we find Aristobulus, son of Herod of Chalcis, ruling over Armenia Minor and parts of Armenia Major.

Chalcis itself fell to Herod, a brother of Agrippa I, and after his death to his nephew, Agrippa II. Subsequently, Agrippa II gave up the throne of Chalcis in order to rule over the Tetrarchy of Philippus. But Jewish Kings continued to rule Chalcis because in 72 A.D. there is still mention of Aristobulus as King of Chalcis or Chalcidene.

Herod of Chalcis took a keen interest in everything concerning the Jewish people. He was guardian of the Temple and entitled to appoint the High-Priests. On the other hand, Herod of Chalcis and his successors had no need to heed Jewish susceptibilities and invariably struck coins[40,41] bearing their portraits.

The youthful portrait of Herod of Chalcis (Nos. 68 and 69) is striking in its strong and not unintelligent expression. The mouth particularly indicates energy. On coin No. 70, apparently struck at a more advanced age, the nose appears larger and more bent, and the expression far more spiritual.[41] We realise something of the energy of this King, when we read that immediately after his brother's death he had Silas executed, whom Agrippa I had spared.[42] Apparently Herod too shared his brother's dreams of independence, since he attended the famous conference at Tiberias.[43] On the occasion of Claudius' ascent to the throne, he too rendered him signal service and therefore called himself "Friend of Claudius".

7. ARISTOBULUS OF CHALCIS (A.D. 57-92).

We are struck by the peculiar and strongly bent big nose, the family trait of the Herodians (Nos. 71 and 72). The forehead is low. The narrow-lipped mouth in particular has an unpleasant expression.[44] Following the usage of the Roman Emperors, this King of Armenia Minor also strikes coins with his

[40] F. de Saulcy, *Mél. de Num.*, III, 1882, pp. 339 *et seq.*

[41] A. Reifenberg, *Portrait Coins of the Herodian Kings, l.c.*

[42] Josephus, *Ant.* 19, 8,3.

[43] *Ant.* 19, 8,1.

[44] A. Reifenberg, *Portrait Coins of the Herodian Kings, l.c.*, where the older literature is given.

wife's portrait. It is Salome, well known from the New Testament,[45] who danced before the Tetrarch Herod and, at the instigation of her mother, demanded the head of John the Baptist. Her first husband had been Philippus, so that she must have been at least in the early forties when this portrait was taken. The face has simple severe lines, not at all reminiscent of those of a "dancer." Unfortunately, the literary sources are silent with regard to Aristobulus! The only fact worth mentioning is that he too stood up to the Romans for his Jewish ccrreligionists.[46]

On the other hand, it seems very questionable indeed whether No. 73 actually represents the same Aristobulus as is commonly assumed. The inscription on the reverse side doubtless refers to Titus and not to Vespasian. If, therefore, the coin was struck at the time of Titus and not of Vespasian, its earliest date could only have been 79 A. D. This, however, would not have been the 17th but the 23rd year of Aristobulus' reign (See No. 72). Moreover, in spite of a strong family likeness, the portrait on the coin shows a different and far younger ruler than the one depicted on No. 72 in the eighth year of his reign, Most likely, therefore, the portrait is that of Aristobulus' son of the same name, mentioned by Josephus.[47] He would have ascended the throne between 63 and 65 A.D. It is highly probable that this ruler is identical with the King Aristobulus of the 4th year of Vespasian mentioned by Josephus,[48] whilst it remains an open question whether he ruled over Chalcis, his grand father's realm, or whether he was King of the region of Chalcidene.

8. AGRIPPA II (A.D. 50-93).

Agrippa's II rule did not extend over a wholly Jewish district; in 50 A.D. he was entrusted with the government of Chalcis, which he in A.D. 53 exchanged for the Tetrarchy of Philip and several other non-Jewish districts. By the favour of Nero some parts of Galilaea and Peraea were added to his state. During the whole of his life Agrippa II was a weak and loyal Roman

[45] Mark. 6,[22] et seq.; Matth. 14[6] et seq.
[46] Josephus, Ant. 20, 1, 2.
[47] Josephus, l.c., 18, 5, 4.
[48] Josephus, BJ. 7, 7.

satellite. From the Roman camp he phlegmatically watched the destruction of the town of his birth. Solely in his youth did he dare to strike coins bearing his likeness. Subsequently Rome apparently forbade any such practice, so that all his later coins show the portrait of the Roman Emperor.

The portrait corresponds to the description of the King found in literary sources. The face is insignificant, the expression effeminate and unintelligent (Nos. 74 and 75). (Contrary to the opinion held by M a d d e n,[49] the likeness on No. 74 shows the portrait to be of Agrippa II).[50]

The various dates occuring on Agrippa's coins are discussed by M a d d e n,[51] M a c d o n a l d,[52] S c h ü r e r[53] and H i l l.[54] On coins Nos. 104-106 the 26th year of Agrippa's reign is equated to the twelfth consulship of Domitian, whereas on No. 103 the 25th year is equated to the tenth consulship.[55] Since however the reading COS X may be due to the bad preservation of the coin,[56] only coins Nos. 104-106 should be considered; since the twelfth consulship of Domitian falls into the year of A.D. 86, the era should be fixed to A.D. 61. Coins Nos. 76 and 77 equate year 6 to year 11 of Agrippa's reign. If the lesser figure corresponds[57] to the era of year A.D. 61, we are able to fix the earlier era to A.D. 56. To this era belong both coins with his portrait, which were therefore struck in A.D. 60 and 65 respectively. It cannot be assumed, that the nomenclature on Agrippa's coins is strictly accurate[54,58,59] and all the Flavian coins should be dated in the later era, the first year of which is A.D. 61.

The coins (Nos. 103-106 of the years 85 and 86 A.D.) show

[49] Madden: *Coins of the Jews,* p. 134.
[50] A. Reifenberg, *Portrait Coins of the Herodian Kings.*
[51] *l.c.* pp. 144 *et seq.*
[52] Macdonald: *Hunter Catal.* III, p. 291.
[53] Schürer: *Gesch. des Jüdischen Volkes,* Vol. I. pp. 589 and 597/8.
[54] Hill: *Catalogue of Greek Coins in the British Museum: Palestine,* pp. xcviii and xcix.
[55] Th. Mommsen, *Wiener Num. Ztsch.* III, pp. 451 *et seq.,* 1871.
[56] A. Reifenberg, *P.E.F. QSt.,* 1935, pp. 81/82.
[57] Schürer, *l.c.* p. 599.
[58] *Ibid.,* pp. 589 anp 597-8.
[59] Th. Mommsen, *Wiener Num. Ztsch.* III, pp. 456 *et seq.,* 1871.

the letters SC (*senatus consulto*) and may be connected with Agrippa's loss of his purely Jewish dominions[61] and the coincident confirmation of his rule over other districts. According to Hill,[62] Mr. Robinson points out that these coins have the inverted die-position, which was the rule in Rome at the time. It may therefore be possible, that they were not actually struck in Judaea, or by Agrippa's authority (?). The legend SALVTI AVGVSTI occurs, as Madden remarks, on the coins issued at Rome in the 10th and 11th consulship and on a very rare coin of the 12th consulship.

Coin No. 90 published here for the first time clearly shows, that the base on which the goddess stands is in reality, the prow of a vessel. Whether or not the coins published by Hill, (*l. c.* p. 239, No. 5 and p. 247, No. 62) should be attributed to Agrippa, is doubtful.

THE PROCURATORS

The Procurators sent to Judaea after the deposition of Archelaus and those who came to the country after the death of Agrippa I, did not strike any coins with signs offensive to Judaism. We only meet with fruits of the country, vessels, arms etc. and instead of the portrait of the ruling Emperor, only his name is given. The coins under Augustus were struck according to the Actian era as shown by Pick[1] and Hill.[2] Since the first coins were struck in the 36th year of Augustus (No. 118), which equals 758/759 a.u.c. or A.D. 5/6, they may have been issued by Coponius, who arrived in Caesarea in the autumn of the year 6 A.D. Kennedy[3] proposes to connect a certain number of the issues with the arrival of a new govrenor. Thus the second set of coins suggests the arrival of Marcus Ambibulus (or Ambivius), the coins of A.D. 15/16 that of Valerius Gratus and the coin struck in the fifth year of Nero (No. 136) may indicate the arrival of Porcius Festus before October A.D.

---

[61] Schürer, *l. c.* (57).   [62] Hill, *l. c.* (59).

[1] Pick, *Ztschr. f. Numismatik,* XIV, 1887, pp. 306-308.

[2] Hill, *l.c.* p. ci.

[3] A. R. S. Kennedy, *P.E.F. QSt.* 1915, p. 198.

59. It may be mentioned that there is apparently no evidence for coins struck in the 33rd year of Augustus,[4] an assumption which misled Mommsen[5] and Madden[6] into believing that these coins were struck according to the era of the "Anni Augusti".

THE FIRST REVOLT (66-70 A.D.)

Whereas it is still uncertain whether the bronze-shekels (Nos. 4-6) should be attributed to Simon, or to the First Revolt[1] the dating of the silver shekels once the "crux" of Jewish numismatics is now definitely settled.

De Saulcy[2] at first attributed these coins to the period of Alexander the Great and later[3] even to the time of Ezra and Nehemia. Reinach[4] thought them first to belong to the First Revolt but later retracted in favour of the Maccabean period.[5] Levy,[6] Madden,[7] Merzbacher,[8] and Rogers,[9] assigned the shekels to the Maccabean period. Hill,[10] following the suggestion put forward by Ewald,[11] and Schürer,[12] attributed the shekels to the First Revolt against Rome A.D. 66-70, basing his conclusion mainly on epigraphic grounds. He tries to show, but only with regard to the letters "aleph", "beth" 'he" and "waw", that if Jewish coins be arranged in the probable sequence of epigraphic development, the shekels could best be placed in the period of the First Revolt. This is surely not

[4] Pick, l. c.
[5] Th. Mommsen: *Gesch. d. römischen Münzwesens*, 1860, p. 719.
[6] Madden, *l.c.* p. 174.

[1] cf. pp.10 *et seq.*
[2] F. De Saulcy: *Recherches sur la Numismatique Judaique* 1854.
[3] F. De Saulcy; *Revne Archéologique*, N. S. 1872, p. 1.
[4] Th. Reinach: *Les Monnaies Juives*, 1887.
[5] Th. Reinach· *Jewish Coins*, 1903.
[6] M. A. Levy *Geschichte der jüdischen Münzen*, 1862.
[7] F. W Madden. *Coins of the Jews*, 1881.
[8] E. Merzbacher, *Z. f. Num.*, Vol. V, 1878, p. 151, and p. 292.
[9] E. Rogers: *A Handy Guide to Jewish Coins*, 1914.
[10] G. F. Hill: *Cat. of Greek Coins in the British Museum: Palestine*, 1914, p. xciii.
[11] Ewald, *Göttinger Nachrichten*, 1855, p. 109.
[12] E. Schürer: *Gesch. d. jüd. Volkes*, I, 1901, p. 761.

correct as far as the letter "he" is concerned. There are many coins of John Hyrcanus with the same form of "he" which we find on the shekels (cf. No. 18a). As we have pointed out before,[13] the ancient script was still used for coinage and similar special purposes, although the so-called square script had already come into general use. One should therefore speak not of an epigraphic development but only of an imitation of earlier forms. There is, in fact, a close epigraphic resemblance between these shekels and inscriptions of the 8th to 6th centuries B.C.

In a paper published in 1927 the author too had tried to show for what archaeological and historical reasons the shekels should be attributed to the Maccabean period.[14] On the other hand G.F. Hill[15] was kind enough to draw the author's attention to a find made by Père Germer-Durand[16] during excavations in Jerusalem. Unfortunately, P. Germer-Durand died before a detailed account of the find was given, but undoubtedly shekels were found here in association with Herodian and procuratorial coins. Discounting possibilities of intrusion, the shekels should more likely be attributed to the First Revolt. Another find which G. Hill has described[17,18] was unhappily not conclusive, Here shekels of the year 3 are said to have been found in association with a Ptolemaic tetradrachm of 285 B.C.(!) and Tyrian shekels dating from between B.C. 126/125 to A. D. 19/20. Both Jewish and Tyrian shekels were offered for sale at about the same time, but there is no evidence that they were actually found together.[19] All the available evidence is against this assumption, a fact further strengthened by the complete difference of the patina, to which Hill also draws due attention.

[13] A. Reifenberg: *PEF QSt*, 1927, p. 47.

[14] A. Reifenberg, *l.c.*

[15] G. F. Hill, *Numismatic Chronicle*, 1922, p. 133-4.

[16] R. P. Germer-Durand, *Revue Biblique*, 1914, pp. 234 *et seq.*

[17] G. F. Hill, *QDAP*, VI, 1936, pp. 78 *et seq.*

[18] G. F. Hill, *Num Chron.* XVII, Ser. V., 1937, pp. 143 4, and *QDAP*, VII, 1938, p. 63.

[19] This view is confirmed by the Rev. Père N. Van der Vliet of St. Anne's, Jerusalem, who told me quite definitely that the coins were not found together.

In the meantime new evidence has been forthcoming[20,21] and because of the importance of the shekels for Jewish numismatics a description of a hoard published by the author[20] is included in this monograph.

The pyxis and coins described here (Pl. XVI) were acquired in October 1940. Here again unhappily no strictly archaeological evidence is available, but there is no reason to doubt the statement of the dealer that the pyxis containing the coins was actually found at or near Silwan, the ancient Shiloah. It may be mentioned in this connexion that neither the peasant, who sold the pyxis to the dealer, nor the latter himself attached any great monetary value to the pyxis. Most of the Tyrian coins, and two of the shekels, show the same kind of green patina as the interior of the pyxis. When bought, this was partly covered with the yellowish-brown loam characteristic of the hill-side near Jerusalem. When acquiring pyxis and coins I was told by the dealer that he had already sold some well-preserved shekels of the same find. These shekels, as I later ascertained, all belonged to year 2.

The *pyxis* (Pl. XVI) is of bronze and has acquired a beautiful greenish-blue patina. Its diameter is 7.5 cm., and its height including the lid is 9 cm. The cover of the pyxis has a pierced handle. The workmanship is excellent, and the cover fits perfectly, which probably accounts for the good preservation of the coins. The pyxis rests on a moulded ring base at the circumference, and the bottom is reinforced by a sort of metal stud riveted to the centre.

Pottery pyxides similar to ours, i.e. with concave sides and lid provided with a knob, were common in Greece in the sixth[22] and fifth[23] centuries B.C. and their origin is said to go back to the geometric period.[24] Pyxides made of various materials were in use in the Roman, Byzantine, and even Umayyad periods. In Roman times they were made of horn, ivory, tin, lead, silver,

[20] A. Reifenberg, *QDAP*, XI, pp. 83 *et seq*. 1944.
[21] E. L. Sukenik, *Kedem* I, pp. 12 *et seq*. 1942.
[22] H. Payne : *Necrocorinthia*, p. 332.
[23] G. Richter : *Shapes and names of Athenian vases*, figs. 137-45.
[24] B. M. *Cat. of Vases*, III, p. 17.

or gold; Pliny[25] in particular mentions pyxides made of brcnze Their use was to hold medicines, toilet articles, or valuables; sometimes even poison, as we learn from Josephus.[26] The latter reference is important as it shows that in the period we are dealing with the Jews were well acquainted with this type. Whether or not the present pyxis is to be attributed to Jewish workmanship is hard to decide. The absence of any figured ornament such as is commonly found on Roman bronze vessels of the period at least makes it possible that we have before us a local product.

The range of the Tyrian shekels in this hoard, from 13/12 B.C. to A.D. 64/65, is consistent with Josephus' reference to Tyrian money current in Palestine at the time of the First Revolt.[27]

In view of the excellent state of preservation of the Jewish shekels and the improbability of any coin remaining in circulation for two centuries, the shekels cannot date from the Maccabean period. It is therefore evident that they belong to the First Revolt. The hitherto unpublished Tyrian shekel No. 7 proves that the issue of full shekels did not stop in A.D. 56.[28] The almost mint condition of this Tyrian shekel, and of the Jewish shekels of the year 2 (A.D. 67/68), proves that the coins were deposited shortly after the issue of the latter. Since no shekels of year 3 (A.D. 68/69) were found, it is safe to assume that the pyxis containing the coins was hidden in A.D. 67/68, about two years before the destruction of Jerusalem.

On the shekels of the first year the name of Jerusalem is rendered ירושלם as against ירושלים on the later shekels. No conclusion can be drawn from this fact, since both ways of writing occur in the Bible.

It will be observed that the chalice is here described as having a cover and not a rim of pearls. Especially the observation of No. 137 leads to this conclusion. It is the cup used for wine-libation which according to the Mishnah[29] had to be covered

---

[25] *Hist. Nat.* XXVIII, 18, 76.

[26] *Ant.* XVII, 4, 2(77) and *BJ.* I, 30, 7 (598).

[27] *BJ.* II, 21, 2 (592).

[28] B. M. C. *Phoenicia*, p. 249, No. 211.

[29] Suk. 4: 10; Ter. 8: 4.

at all times. It might, at the same time, have had a symbolic significance as the "cup of salvation"[30] which was raised during offering. The cup should be compared to a similar one on the door-lintel of a Jewish house at Nave.[31] In all probability the chalice used in the Holy Communion of the Church is derived from this cup. The flowers on the reverse are pomegranates as shown by Narkiss[32] and Romanoff,[33] the latter drawing attention to a passage in the Mishnah supporting this view.

It may be mentioned that the shekel of year 5 is of the utmost rarity and badly struck, probably owing to the precarious situation of the insurgents. The weight of these shekels according to the find of uncirculated coins published by Hill is 14.27 gr. on the average and represents the so-called Phoenician unit,[34] in accordance with the tradition of the Tosephta, which expressly states that: "all the money of which the law speaks is Tyrian money" Not only was the "Half Shekel" for the temple-dues to be paid in Tyrian money,[35] but as the Talmud especially orders, the five shekels which had to be paid as redemption of the first-born were also to be of Tyrian weight.[36]

A coin, No. 146, published by Hill[37] but said to be not of absolutely undoubted authenticity, may represent a quarter shekel of the fourth year; it clearly shows the influence of the Herodian and Procuratorial coinage.

The small bronze coins (Nos. 147 and 148) are usually attributed to the First Revolt, although no conclusive evidence had hitherto been available. Coin No. 147a, which is over-struck over a coin of Agrippa I (No. 59). clearly shows that it was struck after A,D. 44, i.e. at the time of the First Revolt.[38] It may be mentioned, that the representation of an amphora

[30] Ps. 116: 13, 14.

[31] A. Reifenberg: *Denkmäler d. jüd. Antike*, 1937, Pl. 33: 1.

[32] M. Narkiss: *Coins of Palestine*, Part I, pp. 63 and 118, 1936 (Hebrew).

[33] P. Romanoff: *Jewish Symbols on Ancient Jewish Coins*, 1944, pp. 51 et seq.

[34] Head: *Historia Numorum*, pp. 797 and 800.

[35] *Ketuboth*, XII, fin.

[36] *Bechoroth*, VIII, 7.

[37] Hill, *l. c.* (10) p. cjj.

[38] A. Reifenberg, *PEF QSt*, 1935, p. 83

very similar to that on the coins also occurs on a Jewish ossuary found in Jerusalem.[39]

JUDAEA CAPTA

Although not strictly belonging to Jewish series, the coins commemorating the subjection of Judaea are given here for reason of convenience, but only so far as they seem to have been issued in Palestine.

It will be observed that the coins of Vespasian and Titus are struck in Greek, whereas the coins of Domitian show Latin inscriptions. One coin (No. 157) describes Domitian as IMP. XXIII COS. XVI in the twelfth year of his tribunician power, which is never the case on coins struck in Rome as pointed out by Hill.[40] These coins were probably struck in the same year as the coins with the twenty-second imperatorship under the assumption that a twenty-third acclamation would ensue in the next year. It is noticeable that on these coins, as on the coins struck in Rome, there appears the palm-tree, the symbol of Judaea. An unknown variety of the *Judaea capta* coins (No. 158) was published by the author in 1935.[41]

SECOND REVOLT OF THE JEWS (A.D. 132-135).

We know since Hamburger's[1] publication of the hoard found at Dura, near Hebron (not Bittir, as Hill.[2] erroneously states). that all the coins with the names of Simon, Eleazar or Jerusalem have to be attributed to the Second Revolt. Quite apart from other reasons, this is proved by the mere fact that these coins are frequently overstruck over Roman coins ranging from Nero to Hadrian.

De Saulcy wanted to assign these coins to Simon the son of the Patriarch Gamliel II, the Simon Nasi mentioned

---

[39] A. Reifenberg, *Denkmäler der jüd. Antike,* 1937, Plate 18.

[40] Hill, *l. c.* p. ciii.

[41] A. Reifenberg, *PEF Qu. St.* 1935, p. 83.

[1] L. Hamburger, *Ztschr. f. Num. Nm.* XVIII, 1892, pp. 241 *et seq.*

[2] Hill, *l. c.,* pp. civ *et seq.*

on the coins, and not to Bar-Kochba, the leader of the revolt
(The personal name of Bar-Kochba is not known to us). Simon,
son of Gamliel, was president of the Bet-Din and died about A. D.
163. Hamburger agrees with this view, whereas Schürer[3]
considers Hambu ger's combinations to be absolutely false,
inasmuch as Simon's alleged dignity of Nasi is but a legend.

Since the Talmud mentions "coins of Bar-Kosiba",[4] it is
most probable that the coins were really struck on the authority
of Bar-Kochba.

It is much more difficult to identify the Priest Eleazar,
mentioned alone or in combination with Simon on some of the
coins. Without recording all the suggested identifications, we
agree with Hamburger,[5] that most probably R. Eleazar ben
Azaria is the "Eleazar ha Cohen," found on the coins. This
Eleazar was for some time President of the Beth-Din in place
of Gamliel II, father of Simon, and we know him to have been
the descendant of an old and noble priestly family. It is quite
possible that Eleazar served for some time as Simon's guardian,
the latter being too young to act de facto as representative of
the house of Hillel. We have been able to show,[6] however, that
Schürer's[7] explanation shared by Hill,[8] as to the changes
of the names Simon and Eleazar occurring on these coins can
no longer be accepted. There exist coins of Eleazar of the first
and second year and without date (Nos. 169, 170, 189, 196).
The same is true of the coins of Simon Nasi (Nos. 190, 192,
193, 199 with regard to the first and second year) and of the
coins bearing the name of Jerusalem. A hitherto unpublished
coin of the first year of the palm-tree and bunch-of-grapes type
with the name of Jerusalem is given under No 195.

The chronological sequence of these coins is most difficult
to determine, though most authors agree that the undated
coins were the last to be struck. This view is furthermore

---

[3] Schürer, l. c., p. 684.
[4] Tosephta, Maaser sheni, I, 6; Baba kamma. 97. etc.
[5] Hamburger, l. c.
[6] A. Reifenberg, PEF Qu. Stat., 1935, pp. 83-84.
[7] Schürer, l. c . p. 769.
[8] Hill, l. c. p. cv

supported by the fact that there exist hybrid coins of years 1
and 2 (Nos. 171 and 172) and that there is equally a hybrid
coin showing on the obv. Year 2 and on the rev. "l'cheruth Jerusalem' (No 201). It may well have happened that at the beginning of the new year a die of the preceding year was erroneously employed. This would explain the presence of both hybrid
types and prove in addition that the undated coins were issued
in the third year of the revolt. This view is further strengthened
by the fact that there exist no hybrid coins of the presumed
year 3 and year 1.

Let us now consider the motives for issuing undated coins
bearing the name of Jerusalem, instead of Israel. It is known
that Jerusalem was captured by the insurgents[9] and probably
recaptured by the Romans at the end of the revolt, the insurgents withdrawing to Bethar (Bittir), situated nearby. Now there
could only have been an era of freedom during the time the
insurgents were in actual possession of Jerusalem. We therefore find the inscription "Redemption (or freedom) of Israel"
only on the coins of the first and second year. There was no
"freedom of Israel" after the loss of Jerusalem. for all the en-
ergies of the insurgents were concentrated on the recapture of
the city. For this reason there is no date on the coins of the
third year. but only an inscription pointing to the most essential
object of the war. The inscription "l'cheruth Jerusalem" means
"For the Freedom of Jerusalem," commemorating the ardent desire
of the insurgents.

Simply for reasons of convenience we follow Hill in dividing
the coins into tetradrachms, denarii and bronze-coins in the
catalogue.

The reverse of the tetradrachms shows lulab and ethrog,
used in the feast of Tabernacles. We previously met with these
symbols on the coins attributted to Simon Maccabi, and it may
be pointed out that they are frequently represented in ancient
synagogal art. We meet with representations of lulab and ethrog
on paintings and mosaics of synagogues, on lamps and glasses.[10]

---

[9] Schürer, *l. c.*, p. 691.
[10] A. Reifenberg, *Denkmäler der jüdischen Antike*, Berlin, 1937.

Especially should the representation of a lulab found on a column of the ancient synagogue at Nave[11] be compared with the lulab on the coins.

The representation on the obverse of the tetradrachms has caused many discussions. Levy[12] and Merzbacher[13] thought the building represented the Temple, whereas Graetz[14] considered it to be a tabernacle. Cavedoni[15] first thought the building to be the "Beautiful Gate of the Temple", a view to which Madden and others agree.[16] Rogers[17] suggested that the building represented the four pillars for the veil before the Holy of Holies in the Tabernacle, with a conventionalised representation within of the Ark and Mercy Seat, an identification with which Hill[18] agrees. Lambert[19] draws attention to the fact that the chest between the columns is of a type known in Egypt from the Old Kingdom onwards and quite recently H. Rosenau[20] considered this chest to be a representation of the Mercy Seat in the Temple. Some ninety years ago, however, Cavedoni[21] proposed to see in the type the sacrarium of a synagogue, the middle being the ark containing the sacred books, an identification which comes remarkably near the truth.

Comparing the coin with representations of "Thora-shrines" on synagogue-mosaics, ossuaries, gilt glasses, etc. the author has come to the conclusion,[22] that Cavedoni was right in his identification. We see on this coin the front of the Temple Bar-Kochba's followers intended to build, and into the interior of

[11] L. A. Mayer and A. Reifenberg, *The Synagogue of Eshtemoa, JPOS* XIX pp. 314 *et seq.* 1939.

[12] M. A. Levy, *Geschichte der jüdischen Münzen*, 1862, p. 92.

[13] *Ztschr. f. Num.*, I, 1874, pp. 166 *et seq.*

[14] Graetz, *Num. Chron.* Vol. VIII, Ser. 3, pp. 166 *et seq.*

[15] Cavedoni, *Bibl. Numismatik* I, Hannover 1855, p. 34.

[16] Madden, *l. c.*, p. 202.

[17] E. Rogers, *Num. Chron.*, 1911, pp. 205 *et seq.*

[18] Hill, *l. c.*, p. cvi.

[19] QDAP, I, p. 69.

[20] H. Rosenau, *PFF Quart. Stat.* 1936, p. 158.

[21] Cavedoni, *l. c.*, II, 1856, p. 65.

[22] A. Reifenberg, *JPOS*, XI, 1931, pp. 51 *et seq*

which a shrine containing the scrolls of the Law is put. In the same way heathen images are represented on contemporary Roman coins. The horizontal lines inside the shrine indicate the shelves and the two points are meant to represent the scrolls of the Law. J. C. Sloane[23] by comparing the coin with a fresco from Dura-Europos came to the same conclusions but considers the two points to be door-knobs.

Similar views are expressed by Pick[24] who describes the building as a conventional representation of a temple by its ves-tibule, the thora shrine appearing in the centre.

Bar-Kochba maintains the tradition of the Maccabees (or of the first revolt. cf. pp. 10 et seq.) in depicting first and fore-most symbols of the feast of tabernacles which so manifestly expresses the joy of deliverance. The ethrog and lulab on the reverse of his shekels need no further explanation. The denars Nos. 169, 173, 181 and 185 show a jug with palm-branch (lulab) The feast of tabernacles, marking the end of the old year and the beginning of the new, was a popular harvest festival at the same time. This festival was connected with a water-libation ceremony. On each day of the feast water was filled into a golden jug at the spring of Siloam From there it was brought in solemn procession to the altar on which it was emptied by the priests.[25] There seems to be general agreement[26] that the vessel on the denars represents the golden jug used in the water-festival. On this day fires were kindled in Jerusalem and every-where songs and music was heard. The priests accompanied the songs in the temple with their instruments, some of which are shown on the coins. Nos. 172, 174, 178 etc. etc.).

The trumpets on Nos. 174, 182 and 186 should be compared with those represented on the Ark of Titus. Besides, fruits of the country such as grapes. palm-branches, palm-trees and vine-leaves are depicted on the coins of the Second Revolt. The amphora with fluted body, narrow neck and curved handles (Nos. 190, 191, 197 and 198) occurs frequently in the decoration

[23] J. C. Sloane, *Jewish Quart. Review*, N. S., Vol. XXV, pp. 1 et seq. 1934.
[24] B. Pick, *Num. Review*, II, pp. 5 *et seq.* 1945.
[25] *Mishnah*, Suk. 4 : 9, 10.
[26] P. Romanoff, *l. c.*, pp. 28 *et seq.* and earlier authors.

of the synagogues. We find it not only sculptured in stone on capitals but also on lamps, gilt glasses, etc. This vessel probably represents one of the oil-amphorae of the temple, with the oil of which the seven-branched candlestick was lighted.

Always showing a character *sui generis* at times of revolt Jewish coinage reaches its highest standard of workmanship at the very time when the last serious rising was brutally crushed. But the modest designs, showing the intensity of national feeling, not only survived in the synagogue-art of the first Christian centuries, but also influenced Jewish art during the Middle Ages and have survived in popular Jewish art even down to our days.

I. THE PERSIAN PERIOD
(Early 4th Cent.)

1a.   **Obverse**

Male bearded head wearing fillet to l. Eye full. Hair partly shown by granulated line and taken up in knot at back. Border of dots. (AR 16 mm; 3.88 grm)

Reverse

Female head to r. wearing necklace (Aphrodite-Astarte?). Hair falling in club on back of neck. Eye full. She wears an ear-ring, which at the same time represents letter "ayin." Inscr. beg. in field r. below "בקע" = "one half." All in incuse square. Chiselmarked.

1.   **Obv.**

Bearded male head r., wearing a turban-like head dress.

Rv.

Owl standing to r., a fleur-de-lis shaped flower to the left; in field r. inscr.:

"יהד"

"Jehud"

2.   **Obv.**

No traces left.

Rv.

Owl standing to r.; in field r. יה יחקיה (?) in field l. יהוחנן or הד' (?)

r. "Hezekiah"

l. "Jehud" (?)

3.   **Obv.**

Bearded male head r., wearing crested Corinthian helmet; border of dots.

Rv.

Male divinity, bearded, wearing *himation* leaving upper part of body bare, seated r. on a winged wheel; his r. is wrapped in his garment; on extended l. he holds a hawk; above יהד "Jehud"; in field r. bald-headed mask l.; all in square of cable-pattern in incuse square. Cf. Hill, p. 181, No. 29.

II. THE MACCABEAN DYNASTY

SIMON MACCABI (143/2–136/5 B.C.)

4.   **Obv.**

Ethrog berween two *lulabs* (bundels of twigs); inscr. around from above.

שנת ארבע חצי

"Year Four — One half"

Rv.

Palm tree between two baskets filled with fruit; from r. below:

לגאלת ציון

"For the redemption of Zion"

5.   **Obv.**

Two *lulabs* (bundles of twigs); inscr. around from above:

שנת ארבע רביע

"Year Four — one quarter"

Rv.

Ethrog. Inscr. from l. above

לגאלת ציון

"For the redemption of Zion"

6.   **Obv.**

Lulab (bundle of twigs) between two ethrogs.; inscription from r. below:

שנת ארבע

"Year Four"

Rv.

Chalice with knob on stem and cover[1] inscr. from r. below:

לגאלת ציון

"For the redemption of Zion"

[1] cf. p. 31.

6a.   Obv.

Lulab etc. as above:

שנת ארבע

"Year Four"

Rv.

Chalice etc. as above but inscription retrograde, from l. below:

זויצ תלאגל :

"For the redemption of Zion.

JOHN HYRCANUS (135—104 B.C.)

7.   Obv.

Crested helmet with visor and cheek pieces.

Rv.

Double cornucopiae filleted; around from l. above inscr.:

יהו ....שהחבר היהדים

"Jehochanan the High-Priest and leader of the community of the Jews"

8.   Obv.

Wreath of laurel; within inscription:

A

יהוחנן

הכהן הגד

ל וחבר הי

הודים

"Jehochanan the High-Priest and the community of the Jews"

Rv.

Double cornucopiae, between which poppy-head.

9.   Obv.

Wreath of laurel; within inscr.:

יהוחנזה

כהנהגדל

וחברה י

הד י [ם]

'Jehochanan the High-Priest and the community of the Jews"

Rev.

Double cornucopiae, between which poppy-head.

9a.

Similar to preceding, inscr.,

יהוח

נזהכה

זה. גדל

/ / / /

"Jehochanan the High-Priest..."

9b.   Obv.

Similar to No. 9.

Rv.

Similar to No. 9, but with the Greek letter "A" in the lower left field.

10.   Obv.

Wreath of laurel; within inscription:

יהוחנן

הכהנהג

דלהחבר

היה

"Jehochanan the High-Priest of the Community of the Jews"

Rv.

Double cornucopiae, between which poppy-head.

11.   Obv.

Wreath of laurel; within inscription

יהו

חנן ־־ ה

זהגד־לר

א ? שחב

- - - -

"Jehochanan the High-Priest and chief of the community of the Jews"

Rv.

Double cornucopiae, between which poppy-head.

12.   Obv.

Palm-branch; four lines of inscr.; two on l., two on r. reading downward:

יהוחנן

הכהנהגדל

וחברה־

־דים

"Jehochanan the High-Priest and the community of the Jews"
Rv.
Flower between two buds (lily ?).

JUDAS ARISTOBULUS (104—103 B.C.)

13. Obv.
Wreath of laurel; within inscription:

יהוד
גכהנגד
ולוחבר
היהור
ים

"Jehudah the High-Priest and the community of the Jews"
Rv.
Double cornucopiae, between which poppy-head.

13a. Obv.
Similar to preceding inscr.:

יהוד
הכהנגד
ולוח - - -
- - - - - ,

"Jehudah the High-Priest and the community of the Jews"
Rv.
Similar to preceding.

ALEXANDER JANNAEUS (103—76 B.C.)

14. Obv.
Anchor; around inscr. from l. upwards:
ΒΑΣΙΛΕΩΣ ΑΛΕΞΑΝΔΡΟΥ
Rv.
Sun-wheel; between the spokes inscr.:
יהונתן המלך
"Jehonathan the King"

15. Obv.
Anchor with a circle, around which inscr.: ΒΑΣΙΛΕΩΣ ΑΛΕΞΑΝΔΡΟΥ
Rv.
Sun-wheel, outside of which an unintelligible Hebrew inscription.

16. Obv.
Half-opened flower; around from l. above inscr.:
יהונתן המלך
"Jehonathan the King"
Rv.
Anchor within broad circle, around which inscr.: ΒΑΣΙΛΕΩΣ ΑΛΕΞΑ-ΔΡΟΥ (!)

17. Obv.
Palm-branch? around from l. above inscr.:
יהונתן המלך
"Jehonathan the King"
Rv.
Flower (lily ?); no inscription.

JONATHAN HYRCANUS II
(67 & 63—40 B.C.)

18. Obv.
Obverse of No. 16 (flower), restruck by inscription of four lines within wreath:
ינתן
הכהן ה
גדל וחבר   (only partly recognisable)
היהדים
"Jonathan the High-Priest and the community of the Jews".
Rv.
Reverse of No. 16 (anchor), restruck by cornucopiae, between which a poppy-head.

19. Obv.
Wreath of laurel: within inscription:
ינתה
כהה
גדלוח
בר - -
"Jonathan the High-Priest and the community of the Jews"
Rv.
Double cornucopiae, between which a poppy-head.

20.   Obv.

Wreath of laurel; within inscr.:

יהו
נתנהכ
הנהגדל
וחבר - - -
די - -

"Jehonathan the High-Priest and the community of the Jews"

Rv.

Double cornucopiae, between which a poppy-head.

ANTIGONUS MATTATHIAS (40–37 B.C.)

21.   Obv.

Double cornucopiae, inscr. beg. on l. below around and between horns:

מתתיה
כהנגד -
חברהיהד - -

"Mattathias the High-Priest (and) the community of the Jews"

Rv.

Ivy wreath; around from l. above inscr.;
ΒΑϹΙΛΕΩϹ ΑΝΤΙΓΟΝΟΥ

22.   Obv.

Cornucopiae, sometimes with bunch of grapes hanging over; around beg. on l. inscr. (mostly incomplete):

- תתיההכהנה - -

"Mattathias the High-Priest (and) the community....."

Rv.

Within a wreath inscr.
ΒΑϹΙΛ
ΑΝΤΙΓ

23.   Obv.

Within a wreath, inscr., reading retrograde:

מת

"Mat..."

Rv.

The seven-branched candlestick; around beg. on r. below and reading inscr.: outwardly BAC - - - ANT

24.   Obv.

Object represented by a horizontal line from which four verticals are rising; no inscr.

Rv.

The seven branched candlestick; around beg. on r. below and reading outwardly inscr.: ΕΩΣ ΑΝΤ

25.   Obv.

Double cornucopiae with ear of barley between the horns.

Rv.

Within a wreath, reading retrograde inscr.:

מתתיה

"Mattathias"

III. THE HERODIAN DYNASTY
HEROD I (37–4 B.C.)

26.   Obv.

Tripod with lebes; in field r. monogram, l. date. Inscription around beg. above:
ΒΑΣΙΛΕΩΣ ΗΡΩΔΟΥ

Rv.

Thymiaterion between two palm-branches.

27.   Obv.

Helmet to r., showing crest aud one cheek piece; on l. date; on r. monogram; around beg. above inscr.:
ΒΑΣΙ [ΛΕ] ΩϹ ΗΡΩΔΟΥ

Rv.

Circular shield; around a wavy line.

28. Obv.

Winged caduceus; around beg. above inscr.: In field l. date, r. monogram

B[AΣ]IΛEΩΣ HPΩΔOY

Γ⌐　　　Ρ
　　　　Ϊ

Pomegranate on stalk with leaf on either side.

29. Obv.

Aphlaston: in field l. date, r. monogram; around beg. above iuscription·

[BAΣIΛ] EΩΣ HPΩΔOY

Γ⌐　　　Ρ
　　　　Ϊ

Rv.

Palm-branch between two unrecognisable ornaments.

30. Obv.

Wreath or fillet, tied at the bottom and containing as ornament two crossed lines: around beg. above inscr. (often incomplete): BACIΛEωC HPΩOY (sic!)

Rv.

Tripod between two palm-branches.

31. Obv.

Wreath etc. as above, but not closed at bottom. Inscr. as above

BA[ΣIΛE]YC HPΩΔOY

Rv.

Tripod etc. as above.

32. Obv.

Similar to No. 31.; around traces of inscr.: HP - BA

Rv.

Tripod (no palm-branches).

33. Obv.

Anchor; around, beg. on r. above inscription: BACI HPω

(Inscr. sometimes more complete, cf. Hill, l. c., p. 224/226).

Rv.

Double cornucopiae with caduceus between the horns. Sometimes above the caduceus, N (see No. 33 a.)

34. Obv.

Cornucopiae; on l. and r., reading upwards inscr:

BACIΛ
HPωΔ

Rv.

Eagle, standing r.

35. Obv.

Within border of dots inscr.:

BACIΛ
EYCH
- -

Rv.

Anchor within wreath.

36. Obv.

Anchor; around, beg. on l. above, and reading outwatdly inscr. (mostly incomplete): [BACIΛ - - H - -]

Rv.

War galley l., with oars.

HEROD PHILIP II (4 B.C.—A.D. 34)

37. Obv.

Heads of Augustus and Livia r.; inscr beg. above on l.: ΣEBA - - ·

Rv.

Temple with four columns and pediment; between columns date (9— A.D. 5/6). Inscr. beg. below:

Θ

EΠI ΦIΛIΠΠOY TETPAP ·

38. Obv.

Head of Augustus; around inscr., beg. above on l.: [CEBACTΩ KAI] CAPI

Rv.

Temple etc. as above; date (12— A.D. 8/9). Inscr.

∟ I B
- - ΠΟ - ΤΕΤΡΑΡΧΟΥ

39. Obv.
Head of Augustus to r. Inscr. around
beg. on l. above: ΚΑΙCΑΡΙ
Rv.
Temple etc. as above; date (16 — A.D.
12/13).

∟ I Ϛ
- - ΤΕΤΡΑΡΧΟΥ

40. Obv.
Head of Tiberius r.; on the neck
countermark, Inscr. beg. above on l..
ΣΕΒΑ - -
Rv.
Temple etc. as above; date (19— A.D.
15/16). Inscr. beg. above on l.:

∟ I Θ
ΦΙΛΙΠ[Π]ΟΥ ΤΕΤΡΑΧΟ[Υ] (sic!)

41. Obv.
Head of Tiberius, laureate r. inscr. beg.
on l. above: [- - CT - - -, API]
Rv.
Temple etc. as above; date (30— A.D.
26/27). Inscr. beg. below:

∟ Λ
- - ΠΠΟΥ ΤΕΤΡΑΡΧΟΥ

42. Obv.
Head of Tiberius r., laureate. Inscr.
around, beg. on l. above:
ΣΕΒΑΣΤΟΥ ΚΑΙΣΑΡΟ
Rv.
Temple etc. as above; date (33— A.D.
29/30). Inscr. beg. on r. below:

∟ Λ Γ
ΦΙΛ-ΤΕΤΡΑΡΧΟΥ

43. Obv.
Head of Tiberius r. around inscr., beg.
below on l. In front of head branch
of laurel:

ΤΙΒΕΡΙΟCCΕΒΑCΤΟC ΚΑΙCΑΡ
Rv.
Temple etc. as above; date (34—A.D.
30/1)

∟ Λ Δ
ΕΠΙΦΙ - - ΤΡΑΡ
ΧΟΥΚΤΙC - -

44. Obv.
Head of Tiberius r.; in front branch
of laurel. Inscr. beg. below on l.:
ΤΙΒΕΡΙΟCCΕΓΑCΤΟC ΚΑΙCΑΡ
Rv.
Temple etc. as above; date (37—A.D.
33/34)

∟ Λ Z
- - ΠΠΟΥΤΕΤΡΑΧΟ (sic!)

HEROD ANTIPAS (4 B.C.–39 A.D.)

45. Obv.
Palm-branch; across field date (33—
A.D. 29/30). Inscr. around, beg. below
on l.

ΗΡΩ - . ΕΤΡΑΡΧΟΥ
∟ ΛΓ
Rv.
Within a wreath inscr:
TIBE
PIAC

46. Obv.
Palm-branch etc. as above; date (34—
A.D. 30/31).
ΗΡωΔΟΥ ΤΕΤΡΑΡΧΟΥ
∟ ΛΔ
Rv.
Wreath etc. as above
TIBE
PIAC

47. Obv.
Palm-branch etc. as above date
(34 — A.D. 30/31). Inscr.
- - ΔΟΥ
∟ ΛΔ

Rv.
Wreath etc.

T

C

48. Obv.

Palm-branch etc. as above; date (36 — A.D. 32/33).

HPΩΔOY - - PXOY

L ΛC

Rv.

Wreath etc. as above.

TIBE

PIAC

49. Obv.

Palm-branch etc. as above; date (37 — A.D. 33/34). Inscr. beg. above on r.:

HPΩΔOY TE

TPAPXOY

L ΛZ

Rv.

Wreath etc. as above.

TIBE

PIAC

50. Obv.

Palm-tree; across field date (year 43 — A.D. 39/40); around inscr.:

HPΩΔHC TETPAPXH

ETO MΓ

Rv.

Within a wreath inscr. (in four lines

ΓAIΩKAICA ΓEPMANIKΩ

51. Obv.

Palm-branch; across field date (year 43 — A.D. 39/40). Inscr. around beg. on r. above:

HPΩΔHC TETP - -

L MΓ

Rv.

Within a wreath:

ΓAIΩ

KAICA

ΓEPM

NIKΩ

52. Obv.

Branch downwards; across field date (year 43 A.D.-39/40). Inscr. beg. r. above;

HPΩΔHC TET - -

L MΓ

Rv.

Within a wreath:

ΓAI

ΩKA

ICA

HEROD ARCHELAUS (4 B.C.–A.D. 6)

53. Obv.

Double cornucopiae: around beg. on l. inscr. HPΩΔHC

Rv.

War galley l. with oars, cabin, stem curving up at bow, aphlaston at stern; above inscr.: EΘNA - -

54. Obv.

Double cornucopiae; around beg. on r. inscr. (mostly incomplete):

H Δ

Rv.

War galley etc. Inscr. above:

EΘN

ᑫA

X

55. Obv.

Bunch of grapes on a branch with leaf. Inscr. above and on r.: HPΩΔOY

Rv.

Tall helmet with cheek pieces and double crest. On l. small caduceus: Inscr. below: EΘNAPXO (No. 55a; EONAXO).

56. Obv.

Prow of war-galley l. Disposed around

it inscr.: Η Ρ ω

Rv.

Wreath, within inscr.: ΕΘΝ

57. Obv.

Anchor; around beg. on l. below inscr.:

ΗΡΩΟΥ (Sic!)

Rv.

Within a wreath inscr.:

ΕΘ

ΑΝ

HEROD AGRIPPA I (A.D. 37—44).

58. Obv.

Head of Agrippa with diadem, to r.
Inscr. around beg. below on l.:

- - CIAEYC ΛΓ - -

Rv.

Agrippa II on horse-back, cantering to
r. In field under the belly of the horse
date (year 2 — A.D. 38/39). Inscr. beg.
above on l.:

ΑΓΡΙΠΠΑ ΥΙΟΥ ΒΑCΙΛΕΩC

|_ Β

59¹. Obv.

Umbrella with fringe; around beg.
above on r. inscr.: ΒΑCΙΛΕΩC
ΑΓΡΙΠΑ

Rv.

Three ears of barley springing from
between two leaves; across field date
year (6 — A.D. 42/43).

|_ S

60. Obv.

Head of Claudius r. laureate; around
beg. above on r. inscr.: ΤΙΒΕΡΙΟC
ΚΑΙCΑΡCΕΒΑCΤΟC ΓΕΡΜ

Rv.

Temple with two columns and pediment, showing two figures in the
foregrou l and one in the background;
between them the cowering figure of
a naked man. The figure to the l.
(Emperor?) wears a short cuirass. The
figure to the r. (Victory?) holds a
diadem in r. hand, with which she
crowns the head of the cowering man
(Agrippa?). In pediment date (year
7—43/44 A.D.) Inscr. beg. below on l.:

|_ Ζ

ΑΓΡΙΠΠΑC ΦΙΛΟΚΑΙCΑΡ
ΒΑCΙΛΕΥC ΜΕΓΛC

60a Obv.

Head of Agrippa with diadem to r.
inscr. beg. below on l.:

ΒΑCΙΛΕΥC ΜΕΓΑC
ΑΓΡ[ΙΠ]ΠΑC ΦΙΛΟΚΑΙCΑΡ

Rv.

Female figure to l. holding rudder and
palm-branch. Across field to r. date
(year 7 — A.D. 43/44).

ΚΑΙCΑΡΙΑ Η ΠΡΟ[C] ΤΩ
CΕΒΑCΤΩ ΛΙΜ[ΕΝΙ]

|_ Ζ

61. Obv.

Head of Claudius to r., laureate. On
r. below counter-mark. Inscr.:

- - CΕΒΑCΤΟC ΓΕΡΜ

Rv.

Temple etc. as above, but date (year
8—44/45 A.D.). Inscr.

|_ Η

- ΦΙΛΟ ΒΑCΙΛΕΥC Μ - -

62. Obv.

Head of Agrippa with diadem to r.
Inscr. beg. below on l.:

ΒΑCΙΛΕΥC ΜΕΓΑC ΑΓΡ[ΙΠ]ΠΑC
ΦΙΛΟΚΑΙCΑΡ

¹ B. Kirschner (*BJPES*, Vol. 11 pp. 54 seq.) wants to see in this type
a mustroow—anchor alluding to certain maritime events in the king's history.

Rv.

Female figure to l. holding rudder and
palm-branch. Across field to r. date
(year 8 — A.D. 44/45).

ΚΑΙCΑΡΙΑ Η ΠΡΟ[C] ΤΩ
CΕΒΑCΤΩ ΛΙΜ[ΕΝΙ]

∟ Η

63. Obv.

The King, head veiled, sacrificing, and
crowned by two females, one of which
is Victory. Inscr. beg on l.:

ΒΑCΑΓΡΙΠΑC ΦΙΛΟΚΛΙCΑΡ

Rv.

Two hands joined together within a
wreath head in countermark. Inscr.:

[Φιλ]ΙΑ ΒΑC[ιλέως]ΑΓ
[ρί]ΠΑ πρὸς τὴν σύγ]ΚΛΗΤΟΝ
[καὶ τὸν δ]ΗΜ[ον] ΡΩΜ
ΑΙΩ[ν] Κ[αὶ] CΥΜ[μαχία]
ΧΙ – ΑΥ

Cf. Mommsen (8) and Hill (9) quoted
on p. 14.

64. Obv.

Head to l. (Caligula ?). Inscr.

- - ΣΕΒΑΣ - -

Rv.

The King in a quadriga to r., holding
sceptre. Inscr. in two lines above quadriga:

ΒΑΣΙΛ ΑΓΡ - -

65. Obv.

Head of Caligula to l. laurate. Inscr.
beg. on l. below: ΓΑΙΩΚΑΙΣΑΡΙ

Rv.

Emperor in quadriga to r., holding
sceptre. Above in field inscr.:

[ΝΟΜ ΙΣΜΑ]
ΒΑΣΙΛΕΩΣ
ΑΓΡΙΠΠΑ

66. Obv.

Head of Caligula

Rv.

Male figure standing, holding a roll (cf.
Madden l. c. p. 136, No. 4).

ΚΑΙΣΑΡΕΙΑΣ ΑΣΥΛΟΥ
ΑΓΡΙΠΠΑ ΒΑΣΙΛΕΥ[Σ]

67. Obv.

Head of Claudius

Rv.

Within a wreath:

ΕΠΙ ΒΑΣΙΛΕ. ΑΓΡΙΠ
ΤΙΒΕΡΙΕΩΝ

(cf. Madden, l. c. p. 138, No. 3).

HEROD OF CHALCIS (41—48 A.D.)

68. Obv.

Bust of Herod to r., Inscr. beg. above
on r.

ΒΑΣΙΛΕΥΣ ΗΡΩΔΗCΦΙΛΟ[ΚΛΑΥ-
ΔΙΟC]

Within a garland inscr. and date (year
3— 43 A.D.)

ΚΛΑΥΔΙ
ΩΚΑΙΣΑ
ΡΙΣΕΒΑΣ
ΤΩΕΤΓ

69. Obv.

Head of Herod to r.. Inscr. around
beg. above on r.:

ΒΑCΙΛΗΡΩΔΗC ΦΙΛΟΚΛΑΥΔΙΟC

Rv.

Within a garland inscription and date
(Year 3—43 A.D.).

ΚΛΑΥΛ
ΙΩΚΑΙΣΑ
ΡΙΣΕΒΑΣ
ΤΩΕΤΓ

70. Obv.

Bust of Herod, laureate to r.. Inscr
beg. above on r.

ΒΑCΙΛΕΥC ΗΡΟΔΗC

Rv.

Within a garland:

KΛAY
ΔΙΩΚΑ
ΙΣΑΡΙ

ARISTOBULUS OF CHALCIS (A.D.57- 92)

71. Obv.
Bust of Aristobulus with diadem to l.
Inscription around beg. on l.:
BACIΛΕΩC APICTOBOVΛOV
Rv.
Bust of Salome, with diadem to l. Inscr.
around beg. on l.:
BACIΛICCH CAΛΩMHC

72. Obv.
Bust of Aristobulus to l. Inscr. around
beg. below on l. Date (Year 8-64 A.D.).
BACIΛΕΩC APICTOBOYΛOY
ET H

Rv.
Within a garland:
NEPΩNIKΛAY
ΔΙΩΚΑΙCΑ
PICEBACTΩ
ΓΕΡΜΑΝΙΚΩ

73. Obv.
Head of Aristobulus to l. Inscr around
beg. on r. below. date (17 — ca. 80
A.D.?).
BACIΛΕΩC APICTOBOYΛOY
Rv.
Within a garland: Inscr. and date (17—
ca. 80 A.D.?).
TITOYECΠΙ CIANΩ AYTOKPAT
OPICEBACTΩET ΙΖ

AGRIPPA II (A.D. 50–93)

74. [1] Obv.

Head of the youthful Agrippa, to l. Inscr. around beg. on l. (before bust date : Year 5—A.D. 60):

[ΒΑΣΙΛΕΩΣ] ΑΓΡΙΠΠΑ
ΑΓΡΙΠΠ[ΕΩΝ or [ΑΥΙΟΥ]
L E

Rv.

Two cornucopiae with a taenia. Inscr. around :

[ΒΑΣΑΓΡΙΠΠ] Α ΦΙΛΟΚΑΙΣΑΡ
[ΟΣ]

75. Obv.

Head of Agrippa II., Inscr. around, beg. below on l. :

ΒΑCΙΛ [Ε] ΩC ΑΓΡΙΠ [Π] Ο [Υ]

Rv.

Anchor, at both sides of which date: (Year 10—A.D. 65):

L I

76. [2] Obv.

Head of City-Goddes to r. Inscr. around, beg. on l. below :

ΝΕΡΩΝΙΑΔ--ΚΑΙCΑ[ΡΙΑΓΡΙΠΑ]

Rv.

Two cornucopiae, between which caduceus. Date: Year 11—Year 6—A.D. 66. Inscr. around beg. on l. below :

ΒΑC ΑΓΡ. ΕΤΟΥC ΑΙ ΤΟΥ ΚΑΙ≍

77. Obv.

Hand holding ears and poppy-head. Inscr. beg. above on r. :

ΒΑCΙΛΕΟC ΜΑΡΚΟΥ ΑΓΡΙΠΠΟΥ

Rv.

Within a circle monogram (date). Around, inscr. beg on r. above (date :

year 6 — year 11—A.D. 66):

ΕΤΟΥC ΑΙΤΟΥ (Κ≍ = ΚΑΙ≍)

With name and head of Nero.

78. Obv.

Head of Nero r., laureate; in front of head, crescent. Inscr. beg. on r. above:

ΝΕΡΩ ΝΚ[ΑΙCΑΡCΕΒΑC] ΤΟ [C]

Rv.

Within a circle. surrounded by wreath.

ΕΠΙ
ΒΑCΙΛΕ
ΑΓΡΙΠΠ
ΝΕΡΩ
ΝΙΕ

79. Obv.

Head of Nero r., laureate; in front of head lituus. Inscr. around beg. on r. above :

ΝΕΡΩ [ΝΚΑΙΣΑΡ] ΣΕΒΑΣΤΟΣ

Rv.

Within a circle, surrounded by a wreath:

ΕΠΙ
ΒΑCΙΛΕ
ΑΓΡΙΠΠ
ΝΕΡΩ
ΝΙΕ

With name and head of Vespasian.

80. Obv.

Bust of Vespasian r., laureate ; around, beg. above on r. inscr.:

.ΑΥΤΟΚΡΑΟ [ΥΕC] ΠΑΙ·ΚΑΙCΑΡΙC
ΒΑCΤΩ. (Sic!)

Rv.

Tyche or City-godess, wearing kalathos, standing l., holding cornucopiae in l., ears of barley in r. ; across field inscr. (date: Year 14—A.D. 74):

---

[1] The description and photo is given according to the Munich Specimen. Another specimen was found by the author at Banyas. the ancient Neronias (Caesarea Philippi) of Agrippa II.

[2] This coin was bought by the author at Banyas.

ETΔI   BΛ
AΓPI   ΠΠA

81.   Obv.

Bust of Vespasian etc. as above. Inscription as above:

AVTKOPAVECΠACI-KAICAPI
CBACTΩ-(Sic!)

Rv.

Tyche etc. as above, but date Year 15—A.D. 75:

ET IE   BΛ
AΓPI   ΠΠA

82.   Obv.

Bust of Vespasian etc. as above. Inscr.:

AYTOKPA.OYECΠA.KAICAPI
CEBACT.

Rv.

Tyche etc. as above, but date year 18—A.D. 78:

ETOY   HIBA
AΓPI   ΠΠA

83.   Obv.

Bust of Vespasian etc. as above.

A [YTOKPAO VECΠA]
KAICAPI [CEBACTΩ]

Rv.

Tyche etc. as above, but date: Year 26—A.D. 86:

ETOV   KϚBA
AΓPI   ΠΠA

83a.   Obv.

Bust of Vespasian etc. as above, but inscr.:

AVTOK OVEC
KAI CEBACTΩ

Rv.

Tyche etc. as above, but standing on pediment. Inscr.:

ETO(sic!) KϚBA
AΓPIΠ   ΠA

84.   Obv.

Bust of Vespasian etc. as above.

.AVTOKP AOVECΠA
CIKAICA PICEBACTΩ

Rv.

Tyche etc. as above, but date: Year 27—A.D. 87. In field l. above, star.

ETOV   KZBA
AΓPI   ΠΠA

85.   Obv.

Bust of Vespasian etc. as above.

- - - VECΠACI - - -

Rv.

Tyche etc. as above, but date: Year 29—A.D. 89.

ETOY   KΘ BA
AΓPI   ΠΠA

With name and head of Titus.

85a.   Obv.

Bust of Vespasian etc. as above. Inscr.:

AYTOKPAOVEC - - KAICAP

Rv.

Tyche, wearing kalathos, standing l., holding in l. cornucopiae and pouring with r. libation from phiale on altar. Date, if any, not recognisable. Inscr.:

- - ΩC AΓPIΠΠA -

86.   Obv.

Bust of Titus r. Inscr. beg. above on r.:

- - - AYTO - -

Rv.

Tyche or City-godess, standing l., holding cornucopiae in l., ears of barley in r. Date: Year 14—A.D. 14. Across field inscr.:

LIΔ   BA
AΓPI   ΠOY

87.   Obv.

Bust of Titus, laureate to r.; around beg. on r. above, inscr.:

AYTOKPATITOC
[KAICCEB]
Rv.

Nike to r., holding wreath in r. palm-
branch over shoulder in l. Across field
date (Year 14— A.D. 74) and inscr.:

LIΔ   BAC
AΓP   IΠOY

88.   Obv.

Bust of Titus etc. as above.
-AVTOKP.TITOC
KAIC APCEBAC
Rv.

Nike to r. etc. as above, but date: Year
18—A.D. 78.

ET   HIBA
AΓPI   IΠΠA

89.   Obv.

Bust of Titus, laureate to r. Inscr.
around beg. in r. above :
AYTOKPATITOC--
Rv.

Tyche or City-goddess, wearing kalathos, standing l., holding cornucopiae
in l., ears of barley in r.; across field
date (Year 19— A.D. 79) and inscr.:

ETOY   IΘBA
AΓPI   IΠΠA

90.   Obv.

Bust of Titus, laureate to r. Inscr. beg.
above on r.:
AYT---PCEBACTΩ
Rv.

Tyche or City-goddess as above, but
standing on prow of vessel. Across
field date (Year 26— A.D.86) and inscr.:

ETO KG BA
-ΓPIΠ ΠA

91.   Obv.

Bust of Titus to r. as on No. 86, but
bust clothed.

AYTOKPTITO[C]
KAICAPCEBAC
Rv.

Nike to r. etc. as on No. 94, but date:
Year 26 A.D.—86 and in field to r., star.

ETO   KG BA
AΓPI   IΠΠA

92.   Obv.

Bust of Titus etc. as above. Inscr.:
AYTOKP.T--KAICAP
CEBAC
Rv.

Nike etc. as above, but in field crescent
and date : Year 27—A.D. 87.

ETO   KZ BA
AΓPI   IΠΠA

93.   Obv.

Bust of Titus wearing cuirass to r.
inscr. beg. above on r.:
AYTOKPTITOC---
Rv.

Nike to r. as on No. 86, but date: Year
29—A.D. 89.

ET   KΘBA
AΓ   PIΠΠA

94.   Obv.

Head of Titus r. laureate. Inscr.:
AYTO--CTOC
Rv.

Galley with oars to l.; inscr. above.
(cf. Hill, l. c. p. c)
BAA ΓPIΠΠA
With name and head of Domitian.

95.   Obv.

Head of Domitian to r., laureate; around
beg. on r. above, inscr.:
ΔOYMI--ANOC KAICAP
Rv.

Nike to l., writing on shield, which
she supports on her r. knee. Across
field date (Year 14— A.D. 74) and
inscr.:

LIΔ BAC
AΓ PIΠO
Y

96. Obv.

Head of Domitian as above etc. Inscr.:

ΔOMITIANOC

Rv.

Nike to l. as above, but date: Year 18—
A.D. 78, and inscr. around beg. below
on :

ΕΓΟΥ ΗΙΒΑ ΑΓΡΙΠΠΑ

97. Obv.

Head of Domitian, laureate to r.; around,
beg. above on r., inscr.:

ΔΟΜ---ΚΑΙCΑΡ

Rv.

Galley with oars to l. Above date (Year
19—A.D. 79) and inscr.:

ΕΤΟ
ΙΘΒΑΑ
ΓΡΙΠΠ

98. Obv.

Bust of Domitian, laureate, wearing
cuirass to r.; around, beg. on r. above
inscr.:

ΔΟΜΕΤ ΚΑΙCΑΡ ΓΕΡΜΑΝΙ

Rv.

Nike advancing r., holding wreath in
r. and palm-branch over shoulder in l.
Across field date (Year 19?—A.D. 79)
and inscr.:

ΙΘ(?) BAC
-ΓΡΙ ΠΠΑ

99. Obv.

Bust of Domitian etc. as above. Inscr.:

---ΚΑΙCΑΡ ΓΕΡΜ--

Rv.

Nike to r. etc. as above, but date: Year
24—A.D. 84. Inscr.:

ΕΤΟ ΚΔΒΑ
--- ΠΠΑ

100. Obv.

Head of Domitian r., laureate; around,
beg above on r. inscr.:

ΔΟΜΕΤ[ΚΑΙCΓ]ΕΡΜΑ

Rv.

Nike to r., l. foot on a helmet, writing
on shield supported on l. knee; behind
her a crescent; around, beg. below on
l. date (Year 24—A.D. 84) and inscr.

ΕΤΟ ΚΔΒΑ ΑΓΡΙΠΠ[Α]

101. Obv.

Bust of Domitian, laureate to r. Around,
beg. on r. above, inscr.

ΔΟΜΕΤ ΚΑΙCΑΡ ΓΕΡΜΑ

Rv.

Within a wreath date (Year 24—A.D.
84) and inscr.:

ΕΤΟ
ΚΔΒΑΑ
ΓΡΙΠΠ
Α

102. Obv.

Head of Domitian to r. Around, beg.
on r. above, inscr.:

ΔΟΜΕΤ ΚΑΙCΓΕΡΜ

Rv

Palm-tree. In field date (Year 25 A.D.
85) and inscr.:

ΕΤ ΚΕ
ΒΑC ΑΓ[Ρ]
ΠΙ

103. Obv.

Bust of Domitian, laureate. Around,
beg. on l. below, inscr.:

--IVI VEPSF DOMIT--
AVG GER COSX(?)

Rv.

Large square altar with ornaments on
the compartments of the door. Above
and in the field date (Year 25—A.D.
85) and inscr.:

ΕΠΙ[ΒΑ]Α[ΓΡ]
ΕΤ ΚΕ

SALVTI AVGVSTI
S C

104. Obv.

Bust of Domitian etc. as above. Inscr.:

ƷM.CA--OM AVG
GER COS XII
Rv.

Altar etc. as above, but date: Year 26—
A.D. 86. Inscr.:

ΕΠΙ ΒΑ ΑΓΡ
ΕΤ ΚϚ
SALVTI AVGVSTI
[S C]

105. Obv.

Head of Domitian r., laureate. Around,
beg. on l. below, inscr.:

IMCADVESFDO
MAVGERCOSXII
(With countermark)
Rv.

S C; in arc above beg. on l. inscr. In
field below date (Year 26—A.D. 86).

ΕΠΙΒΑΑΓΡΙ
ΕΤ ΚϚ

106. Obv.

Head of Domitian to r., laureate.
Around, beg. below on l. inscr.:

[IMCAD]VESFDO MAVGER
COS XII
Rv.

Two cornucopiae crossed, between
them winged caduceus; in arc above,
beg. on l. inscr.; across field date (Year
26—A.D. 86) and below S C:

ΕΠΙ ΒΑΑΓΡΙ
ΕΤ ΚϚ
S C

107. Obv.

Head of Domitian r. laureate; around
beg. above on r. inscr.:

ΔΟΜΙΤΙΑΝΟϹ ΚΑΙϹΑΡ

Rv.

Nike to r., l. foot on a helmet, writing
on shield supported on l. knee; around
beg. below on l. date (Year 26—A.D.
86) and inscr.

(in field above r. star)

ΕΤΟΚϚΒΑ
ΑΓΡΙΠΙΑ

108. Obv.

Head of Domitian as above. Inscr.:

---ΚΑΙϹΑΡ

Rv.

Nike to r. as above, but date: Year 27—
A.D. 87.

ΕΤΟΚΖΒΑ--ΠΙΑ

109. Obv.

Head of Domitian to r., laureate; beg.
above on r. inscr.:

[Δ]ΟΜΙΤ[ΙΑΝΟϹΚΑ]ΙϹΑ[Ρ;

Rv.

Two cornucopiae crossed, between them
BA. In arc below, date and inscr. (Year
27—A.D. 87):

Β Α
[ΑΓ] ΡΙΠΙΑ [ΕΤ]ΟΚΖ

110. Obv.

Head of Domitian, laureate to r. Inscr.
beg. above on r.

ΔΟΜΙΤΙΑΝΟϹ ΚΑΙϹΑΡ

Rv.

Nike etc. as on No. 107; but shield not
supported and date: Year 29—A.D. 89.

- ΤΚΘ ΒΑ - ΓΡΙΠΙΑ

111. Obv.

Bust of Domitian, laureate to r. Inscr.
beg. above on r.:

ΑΥΤΟΚΡ---ΡΜΑΝΙΚ

Rv.

Tyche standing l. holding cornucopiae
in l., ears of barley in r.; across field
date (Year 29—A.D. 89) and inscr.:

ETO KΘB.
ΑΓΡΙ ΠΠ -

112. Obv.
Bust of Domitian, laureate, with cuirass
to r.   - - ΓΕΡΜΑΝΙ
Rv.
Nike to r. holding wreath in r. and
palm-branch over shoulder in l. Date
(Year 31— A.D. 91) in field and inscr.
below:

ETO ΑΛΒΑ
ΑΓΡΙ ΠΠΑ

113. Obv.
Bust of Domitian r. Around, inscr beg.
on r. above:

ΑΥΤΟΚΡΔΟΜ - - ΓΕΡΜΑΝΙ
Rv.
Tyche, wearing kalathos, standing r.
on base (prow of vessel?), holding in
r. ears of barley, in r. cornucopiae.
Across field date (Year 35— A.D. 95)
and inscr.:

ETOV ΕΛΒΑ
ΑΓΡΙ ΠΠΑ

114. Obv.
Head of Domitian r., laureate; inscr.
obliterated.

Rv.
Nike to r. as on No. 100, but date: Yea
35—A.D. 95. - - ΕΛΒΑ - -

115. Obv.
Bust of Domitian etc. as on No. 112.
ΑΥΤΟΚΡ - - CΑΡΓΕΡΜΑΝΙ
Rv.
Nike advancing r. etc. as on No. 112,
but date: Year 35—A.D. 95.
ETOΥ ΕΛ ΒΑ ΑΓΡΙΠΠΟΥ

116. Obv.
Head of Domitian r. inscr.:
[A]VTOKP - -
Rv.
Within a wreath date (Year 35—A.D.
95) and inscr.:
ΒΑ. ΑΓΡ
ET. ΕΛ

117. Obv.
Bust of City-goddess r. wearing tur-
reted crown; around, beg. on r. above,
inscr.:
ΒΑ. ΑΓΡ
Rv.
Cornucopiae: across field date (Year
34—A.D. 94).

ET ΔΛ

THE PROCURATORS

UNDER AUGUSTUS
Procurators: COPONIUS ca, A.D. 6—9
M. AMBIBULUS, ca. A.D. 9—12
ANNIUS RUFUS, ca. A.D. 12—15

118. Obv.
Ear or barley; around, beg. below, inscr.:
ΚΑΙCΑ ΡΟC
Rv.
Palm-tree with two bunches of fruit;
across field date (Year 36—A.D. 5/6):

L Λ S

119. Obv.
Ear of barley etc. as above.
Rv.
Palm-tree etc. as above, but date: Year
39—A.D. 8/9:

L Λ Θ

120. Obv.
Ear of barley etc. as above.
Rv.
Palm-tree etc. as above but date: Year
40—A.D. 9/10: L M

121.   Obv.
Ear of barley etc. as above.
          Rv.
Palm-tree etc. as above, but date: Year
41—A.D. 10/11:

ᒪ M A

UNDER TIBERIUS

Procurators:
  ANNIUS RUFUS, ca. A.D. 12—15
  VALERIUS GRATUS, A.D. 15—26
  PONTIUS PILATUS, A.D. 26—36
  MARCELLUS, A.D. 36—37

122.   Obv.
Within a wreath inscr.:
          KAI
          CAP
          Rv.
Double cornucopiae, filleted; above
and between horns, inscr. and date
(Year 2—A.D. 15/16):
          TIB
          ᒪ B

123.   Obv.
Within a wreath inscr.:
          IOY
          ΛIA
          Rv.
Branch with eight leaves; across field,
date (Year 2—A.D. 15/16):
          ᒪ B

124.   Obv.
Within a wreath formed of two
branches, inscr.:
          KAI
          CAP
(A coin published by Lambert, Q.D.A.P.,
I, p. 70, shows the inscr.:
          IOYΛIA
on the obverse).
          Rv.
Two cornucopiae, crossed, with cadu-

ceus between: across field date (Year
3—A.D. 16/17) and above, inscr.:
          TIBEPIOV
          ᒪ Γ

125.   Obv.
Within a wreath formed of two branches:
          IOV
          ΛIA
(A coin published by Lambert, Q.D.A.P.,
I, p. 71 and by de Saulcy, Num. de la
Terre Sainte, Pl. III, No. 10 shows on
the obv. the inscr.: KAICAP)

          Rv.
Three lilies: across field date (Year 3—
A.D. 16/17):
          ᒪ Γ

126.   Obv.
Branch of vine, with leaf, tendril and
small bunch of grapes; inscr. above:
          [TIB]EP[IOC]
          Rv.
Kantharos with scroll handles and lid
(lid sometimes missing); across field
date (Year 4—A.D. 17/18) and above,
inscr.:

          KAICAP
          L Δ

127.   Obv.
Branch of vine, with two leaves and
tendril; above, inscr.:
          IOY[ΛIA]
          Rv.
Amphora with lid and scroll handles;
across field date (Year 4—A.D. 17/18):
          L Δ

128.   Obv.
Within a wreath, inscr.:
          TIB
          KAI
          CAP

Rv.
Palm-branch; across field inscr and
date (Year 4—A.D. 17/18):

IOY ΛIA

L Δ

129. Obv.
Similar to preceding:

TIB
KAI
CAP

Rv.
Similar to preceding, but date: Year 5—
A.D. 18/19:

IOY ΛIA

L E

130. Obv.
Similar to preceding:

TIB
KAI
CAP

Rv.
Similar to preceding, but date: Year 11—
A.D. 24/25:

IOY ΛIA

L IA

131. Obv.
Three ears of barley, bound together;
around, beg. below on l. inscr.:

IOYΛIAKAICAPOC

Rv.
Simpulum; around, beg. below on l.
inscr. and date (Year 16—A.D. 29/30):

TIBEPIOYKAICAPOCLIϚ

132. Obv.
Lituus; around, beg. below on r. inscr.:

TIBE PIOY KAICAPOC

Rv.
Within a wreath the date (Year 17—
A.D. 30/31):

L IZ

133. Obv.
Similar to preceding.

Rv.
Similar to preceding, but date: Year 18—
A.D. 31/32: L IH

UNDER CLAUDIUS

Procurators:

CUSPIUS FADUS, A.D. 41(?)—
TIBERIUS ALEXANDER, A.D.(?)—48
VENTIDIUS CUMANUS, A.D. 48—52
ANTONIUS FELIX, A.D. 52—60

134. Obv.
Within a wreath inscr.:

IOY
ΛIAAΓ
PIΠII
INA

Rv.
Two palm-branches, crossed; between
stalks, date (Year 14—A.D. 54); around,
beg. above on r. Inscr.:

TIKΛAYΔIOC KAICA
PΓEPM   LIΔ

135. Obv.
Two shields and spears crossed: around,
beg. above on r. inscr.:

[N]EPΩKΛAYKA
[ICAP]

Rv.
Palm-tree with two bunches of fruit;
across field date (Year 14—A.D. 54);
above and below, inscr.:

BPIT
L IΔ
KAI

UNDER NERO

Procurators:

ANTONIUS FELIX, A.D. 52—60
PORCIUS FESTUS, A.D. 60—62
ALBINUS, A.D. 62—64
GESSIUS FLORUS, A.D. 64—66

136.   Obv.

Palm-branch; around, beg. below on l.,
date (Year 5—A.D. 58/59) and inscr.:

LE KAIC APOC

Rv.

Within olive wreath inscr.

NEP

ΩNO

C

FIRST REVOLT OF THE JEWS
(A.D. 66—70)

A. SILVER SHEKELS AND HALF-SHEKELS
Years 1—5

137.   Obv.

Chalice with knop on stem and cover;
on either side a pellet (pearl?); above
it, date (year 1); inscr. around from
r. below:

שקל ישראל

א

"Shekel of Israel"

"1"

Rv.

Stem with bunch of three pomegranates; inscr. around from r. below:

ירושלם קדשה

"Jerusalem the Holy"

138.   Obv.

Chalice etc. as above

חצי השקל

א

"Half Shekel"

"1"

Rv.

Stem etc. as above

ירושלם קדשה

"Jerusalem the Holy"

139.   Obv.

Chalice as above, with cover but
without pellets; above it date; inscr.
from r. below:

שקל ישראל

שב

"Year 2"

Rv.

Stem etc. as above

ירושלים הקדושה

"Jerusalem the Holy"

140.   Obv.

Chalice etc. as above

חצי השקל

שב

"Half Shekel"

"Year 2"

Rv.

Stem etc. as above

ירושלים הקדושה

"Jerusalem the Holy"

141.   Obv.

Chalice etc. as above

שקל ישראל

שג

"Shekel of Israel"

"Year 3"

Rv.

Stem etc. as above

ירושלים הקדושה

"Jerusalem the Holy"

142.   Obv.

Chalice etc. as above

חצי השקל

שג

"Half Shekel"

"Year 3"

Rv.

Stem etc. as above

ירושלים הקדושה

"Jerusalem the Holy"

143.
Obv.
Chalice etc. as above
שקל ישראל
שד
"Shekel of Israel"
"Year 4"
Rv.
Stem etc. as above
ירושלים הקדושה
"Jerusalem the Holy"

144.
Obv.
Chalice etc. as above
חצי השקל
שד
"Half Shekel"
"Year 4"
Rv.
ירושלים הקדושה
"Jerusalem the Holy"

145.
Obv.
Chalice etc. as above
שקל יש׳ראל
שה
"Shekel of Israel"
"Year 5"
Rv.
Stem etc. as above
ירושלים הקדושה
"Jerusalem the Holy"

B. Silver Quarter Shekel
Year 4—A.D. 69/70
146.
Obv.
Three palm branches (?) or ears of
barley, tied together; in arc below,
beg. on 1 inscr.:
רבע הש |קל|
"Quarter Shekel"
Rv.
Within a wreath of palm-branches (?):
ד
"4"

C. Bronze
Year 2 (A.D. 67—98)
147.
Obv.
Narrow-necked amphora; around, beg
above on 1. inscr.:
שנת שתים
"Year Two"
Rv.
Vine-branch with leaf and tendril.
around, beg. above on r. inscr. (some-
times without ו):
חרות ציון
"Deliverance of Zion"

147a.
Obv.
Similar to preceding, but restruck on
the obv. of a coin of Herod Agrippa
(No. 59), the letters - - BACI - - still
visible. Inscr. beg. above on l.:
שנת ־ ־ים
"Year Two"
Rv.
Similar to preceding, but restruck on
rv. of coin No. 59, the two ears of
barley still visible. Inscr. around beg.
above on l.:
ח ־ י ־ ו ־ ן
"Deliverance of Zion"
Year 3 (A.D. 69—70)

148.
Obv.
Narrow necked amphora with lid;
around, beg. on r. below, inscr.:
שנת שלוש
"Year Three"
Vine-branch with leaf and tendril;
around, beg. above on l. inscr.:
חר|ות|צ|יון
"Deliverance of Zion"

149.
Obv.
Narrow-necked amphora; around, inscr.
mainly illegible:
שנ....לש
"Year 3"

Rv
Cut vine-branch with leaf; inscr. if
any illegible.

149a. Obv.
Similar to preceding, but inscr.:

שׁג

"Year 3"

Rv.
Similar to preceding.

150 [1]. Obv.
Narrow-necked amphora; inscr. if any
illegible.

Rv.
Palm-branch: no inscr.

JUDAEA CAPTA
(Coins struck in Palestine)

A. VESPASIAN
152. Obv.
Head of Vespasian r., laureate; around,
beg. on l. below, inscr.:

Rv.
Nike to r., writing on a shield supported
on a column; around, beg. below on
l. inscr.:

B. TITUS
153. Obv.
Head of Titus, r., laureate; around,
beg. above on r. inscr.:

Rv.
Trophy, at the foot of which to l. a
crouching captive (Jew), to r. a shield.
Around, beg. below on l. inscr.:

154. Obv.
Head of Titus r., laureate; around,
beg. above on r. inscr.:
Rv.
Nike to r., her l. foot on helmet,
supporting shield on her l. knee and
writing on it with her r. hand; on r.
a palm-tree; around, beg. below on l.
inscr.:

155. Obv.
Head of Titus etc. and inscription as
above:

Rv.
Nike etc. as above, but shield hung on
palm-tree; around, beg. below on l.

(on shield; usually illegible
AVT
T
KAIC

C. DOMITIAN
156. Obv.
Bust of Domitian r., radiate; around,
beg. below on l. inscr:
IMPCAESDOMITAVG
GÉRMFMTRPXI
Rv.
Palm-tree with two bunches of fruit:
around, beg. below on l. inscr.:
IMPXXICOS XVICENSPPP
(TR. P. XI. IMP. XXI. COS. XVI-A.D. 92)

157. Obv.
Similar to preceding, but head laureate;
inscr. beg. below on l.:
IMFCAES DOMITAVG
GERMTRPXII
Rv.
Victory to l., holding in r. wreath in l.

[1] No. 151 of the first edition has been cancelled. It is not a Jewish coin.

trophy; around, beg. below on l. inscr.:

INPXXIIICOS XVICENSPPP

(TR. P. XII, IMP. XXIII. COS. XVI-A.D. 93)

158. Obv.

Head of Domitian r.; inscr. beg. below on l.:

- - MITIANVS CAESAR DIVIF - -

Rv.

Victory to l., holding wreath in r.; inscr. beg. above on r.:

VICTORIA AVG

159. Obv.

Bust of Domitian, laureate, to r.; around, beg. below on l. inscr.:

IMPDOMITIANVS

Rv.

Victory to l., holding wreath in r. and trophy in l. hand; no inscr.

160. Obv.

Bust of Domitian, laureate; around, beg. below on l. inscr.:

IMPDOMITIANVSCAESAVG

GERMAN[ICVS]

Rv.

Athena, helmeted to r. on a galley, at prow of which is an owl. She holds javelin in r. and shield in l. hand; behind her a trophy and before her a palm-branch; no inscr.

161. Obv

Bust of Domitian, laureate, l.; around, beg. below on l. inscr.:

DOMITIANVSCAESAVG

GERMANICVS

Rv.

Athena to l. holding shield and spear in l. and placing r. hand on a trophy; no inscr.

162. Obv.

Bust of Domitian r., laureate; around, beg. below on l. inscr.:

IMPDOMIT AVGGERM

Rv.

Trophy; around, beg. below on r. inscr.:

VICTOR AVG

SECOND REVOLT OF THE JEWS
(A.D. 132—135).

A. TETRADRACHMS

163. Obv.

Front of temple or synagogue, showing four fluted columns and architrave; within, in background thora-shrine with shelves and two scrolls of the law; around, beg. on r. inscr.:

יר וש לם

"Jerusalem"

Rv.

Lulab and ethrog; around, beg. on r. inscr.:

שנת אחת לגאלת ישראל

"First year of the Redemption of Israel"

164. Obv.

Similar to preceding, but star above in field to r. and l. inscr.:

שמ עון

"Simon"

Rv.

Similar to preceding; around, beg. below on r. inscr.:

ש ב לח ר ישראל

"Second year of the Freedom of Israel"

165. Obv.

Similar to preceding but small cross above; inscr. in field to r. and l.:

ירו שלם

"Jerusalem"

Rv.

Similar to preceding.

ש ב לחר ישראל

"Second year of the Freedom of Israel"

166. Obv.

Similar to preceding, but wavy line above; in field to r. and l. inscr.:

שמ עון

"Simon"

Rv.

Similar to preceding, but inscr.:

לחרות ירושלם

"For the Freedom of Jerusalem"

167. Obv.

Similar to preceding but star above:

שמ עון

"Simon"

Rv.

Similar to preceding.

לחרות ירושלם

"For the Freedom of Jerusalem"

168. Obv.

Similar to preceding.

שמ עון

"Simon"

Rv.

Similar to preceding, but no ethrog.

לחרות ירושלם

"For the Freedom of Ierusalem"

B. DENARII

169. Obv.

Within a wreath inscr.:

שמע

"Simon"

Rv.

Jug to r.; on r. palm-branch; inscr. beg. above on l.:

אלעזר הכוהן

"Eleazar the Priest"

170. Obv.

Bunch of grapes; inscr. beg. above on l.:

שנת אחת לגאלת ישר

"First year of the Redemption of Israel"

Rv.

Jug to r.; on r. palm-branch; inscr. beg. above on l.:

אלעזר הכוהן

"Eleazar the Priest"

171. Obv.

Bunch of grapes with leaf; inscr. beg. above on l.:

שנת אחת לגאלתישר

"First year of the Redemption of Israel"

Rv.

Palm-branch; around, beg. on r. below, inscr.:

שבלחר ישראל

"Second year of the Freedom of Israel"

172. Obv.

Similar to preceding; inscr.:

[שנת]אחת לג[ואל]תישר

"First year of the Redemption of Israel"

Rv.

Lyre (chelys-shaped) with three strings; around, beg. on r. below, inscr.:

שב[ול]חר ישראל

"Second year of the Deliverance of Israel"

173. Obv.

Within a wreath inscr.:

שמע

"Simon"

Rv.

Jug to r.; on r. palm-branch; around beg. below on r. inscr.:

ש ב לחר ישארל (sic!)

"Second year of the Freedom of Israel"

174. Obv.

Similar to preceding; inscr.:

שמע

[trace of original type]
"Simon"
Rv.
Two trumpets; around, beg. below on r. inscr.:

ש ב לאח[ור] ישר [sic!]

"Second year of the Freedom of Israel"

175. Obv.
Similar to preceding; inscr.:

שמעון

"Simon"
Rv.
Palm-branch; around, beg. on r. inscr.:

ש ב לחר ישראל

"Second year of the Freedom of Israel",
[Traces of previous inscr.:

--KAICNEPTPAI--]

176. Obv.
Similar to preceding, inscr.:

שמעון

"Simon"
Rv.
Lyre (chelys-shaped) with three strings; around beg. below on r. inscr.:

ש ב לחר ישראל

"Second year of the Freedom of Israel"

177. Obv.
Bunch of grapes with leaf and tendril; beg. on l. inscr.:

שמעון

"Simon"
Rv.
Lyre (chelys-shaped); around, beg. on r. below, inscr.:

ש ב לחר ישראל

"Second year of the Freedom of Israel"

178. Obv.
Bunch of grapes etc. as above:

שמעו[ו]ן

"Simon"

Rv.
Lyre (kithara) with three strings; around, beg. below on r. inscr.:

ש ב לחר ישא‎ל (sic!)

"Second year of the Freedom of Israel"

179. Obv.
Bunch of grapes etc. as above:

שמעון

"Simon"
Rv.
Palm-branch; around, beg. on r. below, inscr.:

ש ב לחר ישראל

[--O C-- traces of head of Vespasian?]
"Second year of the Freedom of Israel"

180. Obv.
Bunch of grapes etc. as above:

שמעון

"Simon"
Rv.
Jug to r.; on r. palm-branch; around, beg. below on r. inscr.:

ש ב לחר ישראל

"Second year of the Freedom of Israel"

181. Obv.
Within a wreath inscr.:

שמעון

[traces of original type]
"Simon"
Rv.
Jug. to r.; on r. palm-branch (sometimes missing); inscr. beg. from r. below;

לחרות ירושלם

[Traces of previous inscr.:
-- GER DAC PMT ---]
"For the Freedom of Jerusalem"

182. Obv.
Similar to preceding; inscr.:

שמעון

"Simon"

Rv.
Two trumpets; around, beg. on r.
below, inscr.: לחרות ירושלם
"For the Freedom of Jerusalem"

183.   Obv.
Similar to preceding; inscr.:
שמעון
"Simon"
[Traces of previous inscr.:
-- NERTRAI --]
Rv.
Palm-branch; around, beg. on r. below,
inscr.: לחרותירוש[לם]
[traces of previous type]
"For the Freedom of Jerusalem"

184.   Obv.
Similar to preceding; inscr.:
[ש]מעון
[-- AVGGERM PMTR -- and head of
Domitian to r.]
"Simon"
Rv.
Lyre (kithara) with three strings;
around, beg. below on r. inscr.:
לחרות ירוש[לם]
"For the Freedom of Jerusalem"

185.   Obv.
Bunch of grapes with leaf and tendril;
in field to l. and r. inscr.:
שמעון
[traces of previous type]
"Simon"
Rv.
Jug. to r. with palm-branch on r.
(sometimes missing); inscr. around beg.
on r. below:
לחרות ירושלם
"For the Freedom of Jerusalem"

186   Obv.
Similar to preceding; inscr.:

[שמ[עון
[-- MR -- NO --]
"Simon"
Rv.
Two trumpets between which pellet;
inscr. from r. below:
לחרות ירושלם
[-- ORO --]
"For the Freedom of Jerusalem"

187.   Obv.
Similar to preceding; inscr.:
שמעון
"Simon"
Rv.
Palm-branch; around, beg. on r. below,;
inscr.:   לחרות ירושלם
[traces of previous inscription]
"For the Freedom of Jerusalem"

188.   Obv.
Similar to preceding; inscr.:
שמעון
"Simon"
Rv.
Lyre (kithara) with three strings;
around, beg. on r. below, inscr.:
לחרות ירושלם
[-- RVESP --]
"For the Freedom of Jerusalem"

C. BRONZE
189.   Obv.
Bunch of grapes with leaf; around,
beg. above on l. inscr.:
שנת אחת לגאלת ישר[אל]
"First year of the Redemption of Israel"
Rv.
Palm-tree with two bunches of fruit
across field inscr.:
אלעזר הכהן
"Eleazar the Priest"

189a.   Obv.
Similar to preceding; inscr.:

שנת אחת לגאלת ישר [אל]
"First year of the Redemption of Israel"
Rv.
Similar to preceding; inscr. (retrograde):

אלעזר הכהן
"Eleazar the Priest"

190. Obv.
Within a wreath inscr.:

שמעון נשיא ישראל
"Simon Nasi Israel"
Rv.
Amphora; around, beg. below on r. inscr.:

שנת אחת [לג]אלת ישראל
"First year of the Redemption of Israel"

191. Obv.
Similar to preceding; inscr.:

ירושלם
"Jerusalem"
Rv.
Similar to preceding; inscr..

שנת אחת לגאלת ישראל
"First year of the Redemption of Israel"

192. Obv.
Wreath, in the centre of which palm-
branch: around, beg. below, inscr.:

שמעון נשיא ישראל
"Simon Nasi Israel"
Rv.
Lyra (chelys-shaped) with four or six
strings; around, beg. below, inscr.:

שנת אחת לגאלת ישראל
"First year of the Redemption of Israel"

193. Obv.
Vine-leaf; above, beg. on l., inscription:

שנת [אחת לג]אלת ישראל
"First year of the Redemption of Israel"
Rv.
Palm-tree with two bunches of fruit;
across field inscr.:

שמעון נשיא ישראל
"Simon Nasi Israel"

194. Obv.
Similar to preceding; inscr.:

[שנת א]חת לגאלת ישראל
[traces of previous type]
"First year of the Redemption of Israel"
Rv.
Similar to preceding, but inscr.:

ש מ
[traces of previous type]
"Simon"

195. Obv.
Bunch of grapes with leaf and tendril
around, beg. above on l., inscr.:

שנת אחת לגאלת ישר[אל]
"First year of the Redemption of Israel"
Rv.
Palm-tree with two bunches of fruit,
across field inscr.:

ירושלם
"Jerusalem"

196. Obv.
Bunch of grapes with leaf; inscr. around:

ש ב לחר ישראל
"Second year of the Freedom of Israel"
Rv.
Palm-tree with two bunches of fruit:
across field inscr.:

אלעזר הכהן
"Eleazar the Priest"

197. Obv.
Within a wreath inscr.:

שמעון
[traces of previous type]
"Simon"
Rv.
Amphora, around, beg. below on r. inscr.:

ש ב לחר ישראל
"Second year of the Freedom of Israel"

198. Obv.
Similar to preceding; inscr.:

ירושלם

"Jerusalem"

Rv.

Similar to preceding; inscr.:

ש ב לחר ישראל

"Second year of the Freedom of Israel"

199. Obv.

Wreath, in the centre of which palm-branch; around, beg. on r. below, inscr.:

שמעון נשיא ישראל

"Simon Nasi Israel"

Rv.

Lyre (chelys-shaped) with four strings; around, beg. on r. below, inscr.:

ש ב לחר ישאל (sic!)

"Second year of the Freedom of Israel"

200. Obv.

Vine-leaf; around, beg. above on r. inscr.:

ש ב לחר ישאל (sic!)

"Second year of the Freedom of Israel"

Rv.

Palm-tree with two bunches of fruit; across field inscr.

שמעו[ן]

"Simon"

200a. Obv.

Similar to preceding; inscr.

[ש ב] לחר ישראל

"Second year of the Freedom of Israel"

Rv.

Similar to preceding; overstruck over a coin of Ascalon; inscr.:

ש[מ]עון

[- ACKA -]

"Simon"

201. Obv.

Wreath in centre of which palm-branch; around, beg. below on r., inscr.:

לחרות ירושלם

"For the Freedom of Jerusalem"

Rv.

Lyre (chelys-shaped) with five strings;

around, beg. below on r. inscr.:

ש ב לחר ישרא[ל]

"Second year of the Freedom of Israel"

202. Obv.

Bunch of grapes; around, beg. on l. above, inscr.;

ש ב לחר ישו[ר] אל

"Second year of the Freedom of Israel"

Rv.

Palm-tree with two bunches of fruit across field inscr.:

ירושלם

"Jerusalem"

203. Obv.

Bunch of grapes; around, beg. on l. above inscr.:

לחרות ירוש[לם]

"For the Freedom of Jerusalem"

Rv.

Palm-tree; across field inscr.:

אלעזר הכהן

"Eleazar the Priest"

204. Obv.

Vine-leaf; around, beg. above on l. inscr.:

לחרות ירושלם

"For the Freedom of Jerusalem"

Rv.

Palm-tree with two bunches of fruit; across field inscr.:

שמעו[ן]

"Simon"

204a. Obv.

Similar to preceding; inscr.:

[לחר]ות ירושלם

"For the Freedom of Jerusalem"

Rv.

Similar to preceding; inscr.:

שמעון

"Simon"

204 b and c.   Obv.

Similar to preceding, but barbaric in style; inscr.:

לחרות ירושלם

(Only traces of inscription)

Rv.

Similar to preceding, but barbaric in style; inscr.:

שמעון

(only traces of inscription)

205.   Obv.

Wreath in centre of which palm-branch; around, beg. below on r. inscr.:

לחרות ירו[ש]לם

"For the Freedom of Jerusalem"

Rv.

Lyre (kithara) with three strings; in field to r. and l. inscr.:

שמעון

"Simon"

206.   Obv.

Bunch of grapes with tendril; around, beg. on l. above, inscr.:

לחרות ירושל[ם]

"For the Freedom of Jerusalem"

Rv.

Palm-tree with two bunches of fruit; across field inscr.:

שמעון

"Simon"

207.   Obv.

Similar to preceding; inscr.:

לחרות ירושל[ם]

"For the Freedom of Jerusalem"

Rv.

Similar to preceding; inscr.:

ירושלם

"Jerusalem"

The author is greatly indebted to the curators of various collections for their kindness in placing plaster casts at his disposal.

Coin No. 1 was in the possession of the late Dr. M. Salzberger of Jerusalem. Coins Nos. 2, 44 and 163 are in the collection of the Department of Antiquities at the Palestine Archaelogical Museum, Jerusalem. Nos. 3, 7, 24, 53, 95, 144, 145, 146, 171, 172, 174 and 191 are in the British Museum. London. No. 58 is in the Hunterian Collection, Glasgow. No. 61 is in the collection of the Franciscan Convent of the Flagellation, Jerusalem. No. 74 is in Munich and No. 97 in the Naples Museum. Nos. 39, 50, 149a and 175 are in the Berlin Museum. Nos. 42, 63, 68, 69, 71, 72, 73 and 77 are in the Coin Cabinet of the Bibliothèque Nationale, Paris. No. 85a is in the Beyrouth Museum.

All the other coins are illustrated from specimens in the author's collection.

PLATES

PLATES

Plate I לוח

1   2   1a

3

4   5

6   6a

Persian Period

(Nos. 1 and 2 are 5 times the natural size, No. 1a and 3 natural size).

Simon Maccabi

תקופת פרס

שמעון החשמונאי

(מס' 1 ו-2 הוגדלו פי חמש מגדלם הטבעי, מס' 1a ו-3 הם בגודל טבעי).

Plate II לוח

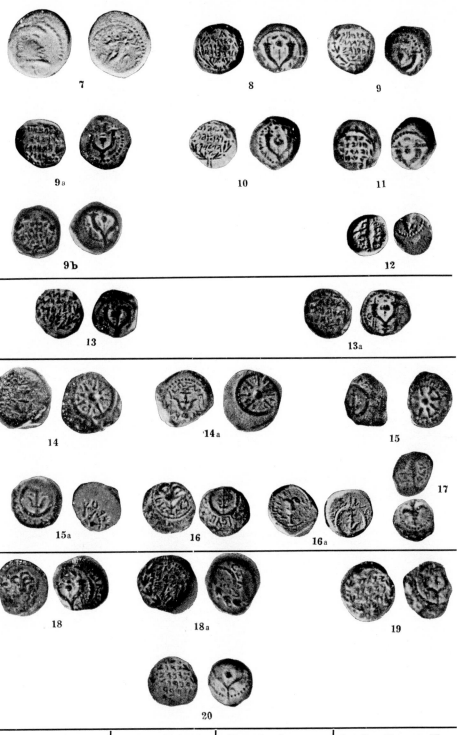

7

8

9

9a

10

11

9b

12

13

13a

14

14a

15

15a

16

16a

17

18

18a

19

20

John Hyrcanus	Judas Aristobulus	Alexander Jannaeus	Jonathan Hyrcanus II
יוחנן הורקנוס	יהודה אריסטובול	יהונתן (אלכסנדר ינאי)	יהונתן הורקנוס

Plate III לוח

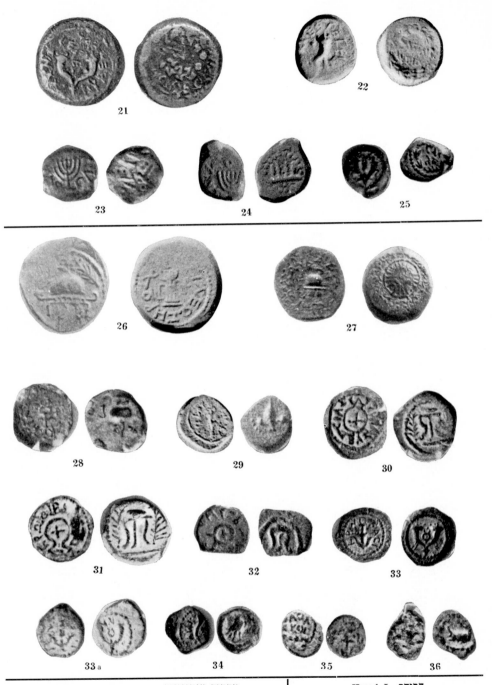

21

22

23

24

25

26

27

28

29

30

31

32

33

33 a

34

35

36

Antigonus Mattathias   מתתיה אנטיגונוס   הרודס Herod I

Plate IV לוח

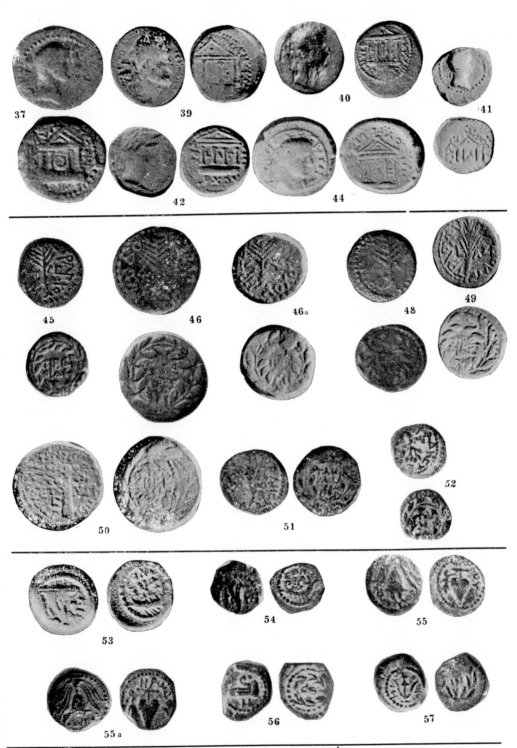

37 39 40 41

42 44

45 46 46a 48 49

50 51 52

53 54 55

55a 56 57

Herod Philip II הרודס פיליפוס | Herod Antipas הרודס אנטיפס | Herod Archelaus הרודס ארכלאוס

Plate   V   לוח

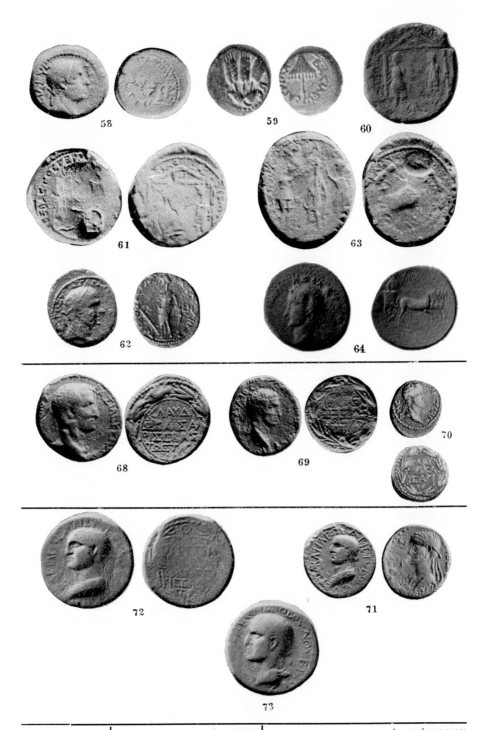

58

59

60

61

63

62

64

68

69

70

72

71

73

Agrippa I אגריפס | Herod of Chalcis הרודס מכלקיס | Aristobulus of Chalcis אריסטובולוס מכלקיס

Plate VI לוח

74   75   76   77

78   79

80   81

83   85 a

84   85

87   89

Agrippa II אגריפס

Plate VII לוח

90

91

93

95

97

98

99

100

101

103

104

Plate VIII לוח

102

105

106

107

108

109

117

110

113

116

Agrippa II אגריפס

Plate IX לוח

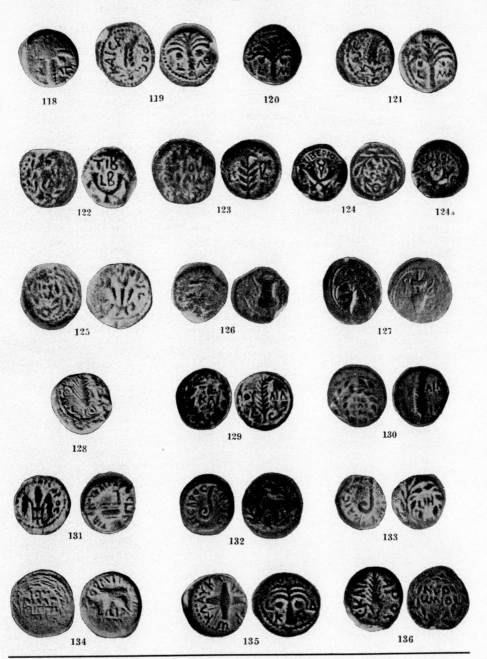

118   119   120   121

122   123   124   124ₐ

125   126   127

128   129   130

131   132   133

134   135   136

The Procurators   נציבי רומא

Plate X לוח

137

138

139

140

141

142

143

144

145

Plate XI לוח

146
147
147a
148
149a
150
149
152
153
155
154
156
159
157
158
162
160
161

Plate XII לוח

163   164   165

166   167   168

The Second Revolt המרד השני

Plate XIII לוח

169 171 172 173 174

175 176 177 178 179

181 182 183 184 187

185 186 188

Plate XIV לוח

189 189a

190 193

192 194

195

191

198 197

The Second Revolt המרד השני

Plate XV לוח

199 202 200 200a

203 204 204a

204b 205 206 207

Plate XVI לוח

1 : 1

אוסף שקלים שנמצאו בירושלים. המטבעות נמצאו
בקופה "פיקסיס" המצולמת כאן.

Date Due